Without Estrogen

Other books by Dee Ito

The Healthy Body Handbook
Women Talk About Breast Surgery
(with Amy Gross)
Women Talk About Gynecological Surgery
(with Amy Gross)

Without Estrogen

Natural Remedies for Menopause and Beyond

Dee Ito

CAROL SOUTHERN BOOKS
NEW YORK

The information in this book is offered to enhance health rather than to diagnose disease or prescribe treatment. Anyone suffering from serious symptoms of menopause should consult an allopathic doctor.

Published by Carol Southern Books, 201 East 50th Street, New York, New York 10022. Member of the Crown Publishing Group.

Random House, Inc. New York, Toronto, London, Sydney, Auckland

Manufactured in U.S.A.
Library of Congress Cataloging-in-Publication Data
Ito, Dee.
Without estrogen : natural remedies for menopause and beyond / by Dee Ito.—1st ed.
p. cm.
Includes bibliographical references and index.
1. Menopause—Complications—Alternative treatment. I. Title.
RG186.I86 1994
618.1'7506—dc20 94-2618
CIP

ISBN 0-517-58825-0
10 9 8 7 6 5 4 3 2

For the women who are going
through menopause without estrogen with
every expectation of staying healthy and
enjoying their lives at every age

Acknowledgments

I am very grateful to the alternative practitioners who generously shared their knowledge and wisdom with me and I thank them for their patience and support: Serafina Corsello, M.D., Melanie Danza, Rebecca Elmaleh, M.D., Marcia Greenleaf, Ph.D, Christine Henrich, M.T., Roberta Kirchenbaum, Neil Kobetz, D.C., Loretta Mears, D.C., Marika Molnar, P.T., Sarnell Ogus, Jeffrey Sullender, Ph.D, C.C.N., Teresa Xu, and my healer.

Special thanks, too, go to Kate Anderson, Marshall Arisman, Amy Gross, Janice Heywood, R.N., Bruce Ito, Rita Marshall, Ted Pankin, and most especially to Margaret Richardson whose generous and unconditional personal support and professional expertise eased the completion of this book.

My deep appreciation and thanks to my publisher and editor, Carol Southern, whose vision for and belief in the concept and value of this book never wavered.

Contents

Foreword

Without Estrogen is unique among the growing number of books recently published on the subject of menopause. Nondogmatic and nondoctrinaire in its approach, *Without Estrogen* offers self-help information in an original format that makes an important contribution to the existing literature on women's health. By combining the views of expert practitioners of alternative therapies with the stories of women who share their experiences in managing the signs of menopause, Dee Ito makes this needed information directly accessible to her readers. There are many self-help books for women, but by framing her book as an adjunct to decision-making, it not only becomes a valuable resource for women but also offers physicians and other health care providers options for their patients who can't, or choose not to, rely on hormone replacement therapy (HRT).

Without Estrogen significantly advances the possibility that women can be healthier as they grow older. At the same time, the book engages the broader historical and theoretical struggle of women in their efforts to regain control of their bodies. Women's health has only been in the province of experts for 150 years. Before the advent of industrialization and the growing influence of allopathic medicine removed the power from their hands, women in many cultures were the healers. They held control over the definition, diagnosis, and management of their own health and that of their community. But the shift in power to allopathic medicine has meant that women have largely lost this role, and particularly when dealing with biologic events like childbirth and menopause.

The benefits to women from advances in Western medicine have been significant. They live longer with less suffering—particularly those women who can afford treatment. This improvement in their quality of life supports a perception that medical intervention in women's normal life processes is necessary. That perception along with today's social climate encourages both women and their physicians to use medical intervention even when medical problems do not exist and limits the possibilities of exploring nonallopathic options. A system invested with the reputation for magic bullets and miracle cures is not structured to consider other directions.

However, significant debate does continue among medical experts about the different aspects of HRT. Recently, Dr. Jerilyn Prior, a noted reproductive endocrinologist* discussed her deep skepticism that "menopause is a medical liability" and further questions whether "estrogen deficiency is the major problem." In the article she writes about being disinvited to author a textbook chapter on osteoporosis because she failed to support hormone replacement therapy.

Other aspects of the controversy within the medical community include uncertainty about such issues as: Who should use HRT? Should estrogen be prescribed alone or in combination with progesterone? What dose is appropriate

*January/February, 1994, *Journal of the American Medical Women's Association*

and in what combination? What are the immediate and future benefits and consequences of hormone replacement therapy? It is precisely because these issues are unresolved that the Office for Research on Women's Health of the National Institutes of Health felt it necessary to launch its large study of hormone replacement therapy.

It is a daunting task for any woman to sort out the risks and benefits of HRT but particularly if she is physically or psychologically fragile or compromised by illness. However, if women choose to conduct a personal risk/benefit analysis with their physicians they should know that the discussion will rarely be unbiased. Physicians—under complex professional pressures—disproportionately value the use of conventional treatments when counselling patients and will often encourage women to use hormone replacement therapy without a full and thoughtful examination of other options. Women should also know that sometimes physicians discuss risk inappropriately by emphasizing the most dramatic possibilities and consequences if a woman fails to use HRT. By adopting the medicalized view that menopause equals disease—rather than seeing it as a phase in a woman's biologic development—physicians contribute to a fear-based environment around the issue. Consequently, HRT is prescribed for every woman as if *all* women will experience such severe signs that they must be treated medically. HRT is also regarded as the only correct intervention for treating menopausal signs. Reliance on this single modality is influenced by the fact that menopausal drugs are sold for significant profit. Under these circumstances, evaluating other approaches or providing information or access to alternatives is difficult. But, even if a physician is open to the discussion, it is virtually impossible for an individual practitioner to know all the therapeutic options for any common condition—some may even be unaware that options to HRT exist.

It is always hard to face a patient who comes into the doctor/patient encounter in distress or discomfort with no good recommendations to improve her health. This is one more reason why *Without Estrogen* is an important resource for open, inquisitive health care providers trained in the allopathic tradition.

As a physician, I remain a pragmatist. I know that what may be a minor symptom to one woman is a disabling event to another. *Without Estrogen* expands the range of interventions available both to me and my patients.

Some readers will find *Without Estrogen* controversial precisely because it challenges established notions of the medical power structure—its expertise and its autonomy. This disputed terrain is the book's great strength. It offers specific information made easily accessible and, ideally, it will be adopted as a supplemental text in medical schools. Certainly it will get wide readership among women. *Without Estrogen* is a profoundly important resource.

Barbara Herbert, M.D.
Boston City Hospital

Introduction

All of us who are in menopause are now in our prime. We have the experience, insight, and maturity to know who we are and what we want to do in our lives. The aspirations and hopes we have did not exist for us even twenty years ago. It was not expected that we would be starting new careers at fifty, running companies at sixty-five, or playing tennis with our grandchildren and even winning. As we age we want the option to have active sex lives. We want to look well and enjoy our vitality. We want to be free from illness. And if we want these things, we can achieve them. We do lead increasingly stressful lives, with demands made on our time and attention from every direction. And with sometimes dramatic physical changes happening in our bodies, we *know* we need help if we are to make the most of this new phase of life.

Though menopause is out of the closet, and women are sharing their experiences with each other, most women find that whatever their problems, the only solution approved by the medical establishment is estrogen replacement therapy (ERT). In fact, medical intervention at menopause is recommended by most physicians. And even though every woman's body responds differently to hormone loss, hormone replacement therapy is generally prescribed in a standard dose—regardless of age—for all women. Alternative approaches are rarely favored by members of the traditional medical community. The women who can't or don't want to take hormones are given very little guidance and are left to get through menopause the best way they can.

Most gynecologists tell us the benefits of taking hormones outweigh the risks—the major benefit being the prevention of osteoporosis. But many women question whether they want to be medicated for the rest of their lives to prevent this condition. They also know that the pharmaceutical industry's track record for developing safe hormone substitutes for long-term use by women is not reassuring. DES (a synthetic estrogen used to prevent miscarriage), early birth control pills with high hormone levels, and even estrogen replacement therapy used without progesterone were researched and pronounced safe. But we know these hormones sometimes produce serious side effects, and we now know they have also caused cancer.

Today, although hormone replacement therapy (estrogen used with progesterone) is considered to be safe, many doctors discourage patients with a family history of breast or uterine cancer from using estrogen. Unfortunately, studies are contradictory or inconclusive not only on breast cancer, but on heart disease as well, and every year there are new studies reevaluating the old studies and new ways of assessing the risks.

In September 1993 the definitive study on the long-term effects of women taking estrogen and progesterone began. Conducted by the National Institutes of Health, the study will take twelve years to complete. Carol Rinzler, in a *New York Times* Op-Ed article[1] on the risks to women participating in this broad-ranging study, warns that "the National Women's

Health Network, a nonprofit organization, predicts that by the time it ends there will be at least 120 cases of endometrial cancer among women who would have remained healthy if they hadn't joined the hormone trial." Further, she quotes from a sixteen-study comparison conducted by the Federal Centers for Disease Control that "found a small but statistically significant increase in breast cancer risk due to long-term estrogen use."

So it is not surprising that so many women are reluctant to go on ERT. In fact, according to *Newsweek,* "only 15 percent of menopausal American women take hormones," and many of those women don't stay on them for more than nine months, according to research from pharmaceutical companies. Evidently a great many of us are not taking hormones. Some of us were told by our doctors that we should not take estrogen, some of us worry about the risk of cancer, others are philosophically against long-term use of any chemical, including hormones. And because synthetic estrogen is generally prescribed with progesterone, the hormone that activates menstruation, there are the women who simply hate the thought of having periods again.

Clearly, messing around with our hormones is serious. Natural hormones affect how we look and how we feel. They affect our energy level and our muscle strength. But are chemical hormones the only real option we have to make sure menopause will not mark our decline? Can we grow older and stay healthy with our hearts and bones strong, our energy vital—without estrogen? I believe we can.

While studies of the risks of taking hormones are few and the major investigative study years away from completion, research and clinical trials on natural alternatives to hormone replacement are nonexistent. However, that does not mean alternatives do not exist. On the contrary, as I have discovered, there is a great deal of information on the subject. There are many books—old and new—on herbs, as well as books on homeopathy and vitamins. Sourcebooks on women's health feature material on alternative medicine. There are also specialized newsletters and pamphlets detailing folk remedies centuries old. And there are practitioners in the alternative medicine field who advocate other remedies. With so much material and alternative treatment options available and so much concern about hormone risk, I was convinced there must be women quietly trying various remedies and using these treatments despite the controversy.

I began asking around, tapping the wide network of women I had drawn from when coauthoring books on breast cancer and gynecological surgery. And I not only met women who were using alternative methods successfully, but I discovered there were many more approaches to dealing with menopause than I had been led to believe. Hot flashes, vaginal dryness, memory loss, sleep disturbances, dramatic signs of aging, and mood swings—all the conventional symptoms of menopause—were being treated with natural remedies and treatments. Some women are using alternative methods until there is more conclusive research on the risks of chemical estrogen. Others have consulted alternative practitioners and are following regimens that will help them stay healthy beyond menopause. Some of the women are using chiropractors and acupuncturists to treat symptoms, while more adventuresome women are reading books and prescribing for themselves.

I decided that women who can't or don't want to take ERT need information in a single sourcebook, not only to get through menopause comfortably, but to use for the rest of their lives. Alternative therapies are not only useful to treat symptoms, but can be adapted and adjusted to meet the needs of our ever-changing bodies as we grow older. I discovered that many of the emotional and psychological complications of aging can be treated with hands-on body work like massage or mind/body therapies like hypnosis, and that the range of alternative treatment possibilities is very broad. But considering alternatives to estrogen replacement is only one part of a much larger trend.

More and more people are becoming familiar with the principles behind natural forms of medicine. Early last year Bill Moyers, on public television, made us aware of herbal remedies used successfully in China and revealed the kinds of serious body/mind exploration going on in this country. He stressed that herbal medicine and conventional medicine were both available to the Chinese, and that the Chinese were comfortable consulting doctors from both disciplines.

In January 1993, while I was in the midst of researching this book, the U.S. government announced the establishment of the first Department of Alternative Medicine to study and research alternatives to chemical and surgical treatments, concentrating on prevention and natural cures. This government support reflects the concerns of a growing number of people, including health care professionals, who are exploring ways to keep themselves and their patients well by using alternative treatments that work with few, if any, side effects. Alternative therapies offer us opportunities to learn to care for our own aches and pains, particularly if we are not seriously ill. We can make a difference in how we feel without total dependence on a doctor. We can learn to use specialists—including medical doctors—as resources to gain a greater understanding of our bodies. Developing trust in the people we pay to give us advice and recommend treatment is different from being dependent on them to "fix us" when we have a problem.

Evidence that this trend is here to stay is seen in the number of health food stores and vitamin and herb shops in large towns and cities. It is also clear that whether or not there is medical approval or research to determine the long-term effects, alternatives are being used alone or in combination with conventional medicine, because they work. People are taking responsibility for seeking out and receiving unconventional treatment with and without their doctors' blessings. And they are willing to pay for it themselves (as medical insurance plans often do not cover alternative therapies). This says a great deal about the limitations of traditional medical systems and the potential of alternative approaches.

Traditional herbs have been used through the centuries, as has hands-on body work like reflexology and other physical therapies. Most of this knowledge has been passed down through generations, and despite medical skepticism, many of these treatments are still used by practitioners today. But even with the long history and effectiveness of these wise, time-tested ways, there is still only anecdotal evidence of results—although the body of evidence kept by alternative healers is substantial.

Early on, practitioners were sometimes unknown even to each other, but today a large community of natural medicine specialists exists across the country. Many professional organizations, institutions, and publications are keeping the public aware of different forms of healing. Therapists and healers have been working quietly to educate patients to heal themselves. They are finding ways to demystify ancient, sometimes foreign, concepts from China and India and to reinterpret and update remedies and treatments. The main ideas growing out of this movement—taking responsibility for one's own body, using natural remedies and procedures, avoiding surgery when possible, and learning how to develop an awareness of what it means to be healthy—have already influenced changes in the conventional doctor-patient relationship.

We must remember that conventional medicine is not the enemy; what it does well, it does superbly. It's vitally important for us to seek medical treatment when it is required and not expect from alternative practitioners what they cannot provide.

I hope this book will help you become more comfortable with and enthusiastic about the idea of using alternative remedies. The treatments and/or programs included here can benefit you—whether you are going through menopause or your menopause has ended—and keep you healthy for the rest of your life. The choice of program is yours, based on your physical needs, career challenges, life-style, and temperament.

Part One

Natural Menopause

Managing Menopause Naturally

Natural menopause is seen by alternative practitioners within the context of a whole body, a whole life. Menopause is the introduction to a new phase in a woman's life, much the same way menstruation marked the passage into adolescence. Our diminishing hormones change the way our bodies look, feel, and respond, and a natural menopause can help us become comfortable with our new bodies. But we have to learn all over again what *is* natural rather than quickly opting for a synthetic intervention to deal with the changes. Alternative therapists approach menopause as a time to balance the body, the mind, and the emotions.

Depending on when we enter menopause, we can expect our bodies to undergo many changes. We can make the choice to be physically fit and emotionally and psychologically flexible. The women I've talked with want to know not only how to get rid of hot flashes without estrogen, but the best natural ways to keep their bones and muscles strong, to increase stamina, to prevent disease, and, frankly, to enjoy the benefits of maturity. Alternative therapies accommodate those aspirations and encourage women to begin personal maintenance programs to keep themselves healthy far beyond menopause.

The program that's appropriate for you depends on your symptoms, your general health, and your life-style. There is no one right way for all women. Each woman's body needs different treatment: some women have frail constitutions, some have heavier, stronger bones, some—due to surgery—do not have ovaries, and some produce natural hormones longer than others. Dealing with the differences is one of the realities of using natural therapies.

Without estrogen, menopausal symptoms can be managed individually. Different herbs, vitamins, cell salts, and homeopathic and other traditional remedies and treatments can help alleviate physical symptoms—hot flashes, night sweats, bladder control, memory loss, uncomfortable skin sensations, and so on. Mind/body therapies like self-hypnosis and massage can help reduce anxiety and stress. A personalized diet and exercise programs can help prevent bone loss and protect women against developing osteoporosis. Heart disease—another major health concern in older women—is one of the main reasons doctors recommend synthetic hormone replacement. But heart disease, too, can be handled alternatively.

The "first nonsurgical, nonpharmaceutical therapy for heart disease" to qualify for insurance reimbursement made front-page news in *The New York Times*[2] last year. The program, developed for women and men by Dr. Dean Ornish, director of the Preventive Medicine Research Institute in Sausalito, California, combines "diet, meditation, exercise and support groups to reverse heart disease," *without* using drugs or surgery. The alternative practitioners I spoke with are very familiar with Dr. Ornish's program. It is a good model, and not only for preventing heart disease; when adjusted and personalized, it can help prevent any illness and maintain health in most menopausal women.

Any good natural regimen for healthy older women works to strengthen the entire immune system to help prevent the development of disease. But the approach is always multi-therapeutic and includes diet, exercise, body/mind techniques, and sometimes supplements—herbs, vitamins, minerals, and so forth. And there is no getting around it: following such a program requires time, particularly at the outset, and demands a real commitment to being well. Incorporating a new regimen into your life may not be easy; the challenge is to find a way to sustain your resolve. Concentrating on the benefits will help you do what needs to be done. To use natural therapies, we need to understand not only that each woman's body is different, but that treatments may take different amounts of time to be effective. Given the proper support, the body can balance itself. Making the care of our bodies a priority means taking the long view. Good health has to be worth it, or there will always be excuses not to exercise, not to eat the right foods, and not to relax. Few of us are lucky enough to be able to take health for granted. Most of us have to educate ourselves to pay close attention to the changes in both physical and emotional needs as we age, and we have to know what to do about them and whom to consult when we don't know. Those needs may shift focus radically from year to year, requiring us to adjust our program to meet our bodies' new needs.

Understanding the effects of the decreasing production of hormones in our bodies is important to deciding on a program of health care. Only surgical removal of the ovaries results in a cessation of hormone production. Otherwise, ovarian hormone production decreases at an individualized rate, eventually slowing to minimal production (usually) in our early sixties. The adrenals, however, continue to produce small amounts of estrogen, progesterone, and androgen hormones. Additional estrogen is stored in the fat tissues, so women who have a little extra fat have an extra source of estrogen.

Premarin, by the way, is not a natural estrogen, even though many gynecologists regard it as natural because Premarin is derived from the urine of pregnant mares. The mare estrogen is chemically processed in the laboratory and is a drug. It works in the body like any other drug. The herbs used to help diminish menopausal symptoms—black cohosh, licorice, dong quai, damiana, ginseng, and so forth—are natural plant roots and leaves that are powdered, decocted (boiled), or infused (mixed with water) for direct use commercially or personally. They have various therapeutic actions. Some have estrogenic qualities, others encourage hormone balance and help stimulate hormone production in the body.

If you *do* take Premarin or other chemical hormones, consider a program of health care that may even help offset any of the negative effects from the drugs you take. It could be worthwhile. Making changes in your diet, like those that women who don't use estrogen need to make, along with regular exercise and even vitamin or herb supplementation can help strengthen the immune system and balance the body.

Menopause is an ideal time to practice conscious preventive care of our bodies. Natural treatment programs for menopause diminish symptoms, but beyond that, the best of them try to determine the *cause* of the symptoms—symptoms that may be connected directly to hormone changes or may instead be related to nutrition or stress.

Far too often, conventional medicine treats symptoms in older people as if the underlying problem is old age. It accounts for the often dismissive attitude doctors have toward us as we grow older—beginning, unfortunately, at menopause. Alternative therapists, on the other hand, see menopause as another stage in the life cycle that demands a different approach to health than do the years of adolescence or fertility.

The Place of Traditional Medicine

Modern medicine is outstanding in dealing with acute medical emergencies like accidents, heart attacks, ruptured appendixes, and burns. But it has not been as successful in the prevention of illness or emotional stress, in dealing with chronic diseases, or in treating the common physical problems that normally plague well people—colds, flus, backaches, allergies, and the side effects of age-related changes.

Alternative therapies, on the other hand, are particularly useful in recognizing and treating predisease conditions triggered by the body, the mind, or the emotions. Chronic conditions that do not respond to conventional treatment often do very well with alternative approaches that work to restore normal body functions. Extreme fatigue, emotional stress, and depression are treated seriously by alternative practitioners because they know that without treatment these conditions can develop into illness. Natural methods take longer to work than drugs, but there are few, if any, side effects. The quick fix—a sometimes necessary advantage of drug therapy—is not in the profile of most alternative practices. Alternative specialists rely on the body's ability to heal itself. This approach works best, however, when the problem has not yet reached crisis proportions, by curing the normal aches and pains and minor illnesses that if left untreated could become serious. Although alternative therapies have been responsible for what appear to be miracle cures, in general there is no clinical evidence that they have been successful in eliminating life-threatening illness, particularly in the latter stages. Alternative medical literature, however, provides many anecdotal examples of success in preventing disease in its *early* stages from becoming life-threatening.

There is a misperception about the attitude most alternative therapists hold regarding conventional medicine. The specialists I've talked with are not opposed to conventional medicine. On the contrary, they often refer clients to medical colleagues if they feel drugs, surgery, or other kinds of therapy are necessary. There is also a growing recognition among doctors that natural approaches may have validity—particularly as nonsurgical, nonpharmaceutical approaches like those of Dr. Dean Ornish are accepted.

Most alternative professionals agree that getting rid of a symptom is only one part of their role as healers. A symptom gives you information about the rest of the body, including the mind and the emotions. That's why a first session with a specialist often lasts from one to two hours—enough time to get to know you—and five to ten sessions is not an uncommon course of treatment. Most practitioners ask their clients to provide complete health histories, which cover such wide-ranging areas as general health problems, pressures, bowel regularity, water intake, food allergies, work and career assessments, family life, and personal life-style—in other words, anything that might influence your body's health. In addition to conventional testing methods they rely heavily on observation and intuition as major tools for diagnosis.

Many practitioners specialize in one method—chiropractic, nutrition, acupuncture, and so on—but have knowledge of or are experienced in other alternatives. They also make it a practice to seek out new approaches, often exchanging information with other practitioners. This is one of the reasons multitherapeutic directions are common in the natural health field.

The origins of these naturopathic approaches to healing date back to Hippocrates, who used a range of natural methods in treating his patients. Early Egyptian, Greek, and Roman doctors approached medicine the same way today's naturopathic physicians do—by using herbal remedies, diet, and exercise as well as other treatments. A growing number of medical doctors like Dr. Serafina Corsello (see page 22) now believe in preventing illness and treating disease through various natural therapeutic approaches. Only medical doctors are able to prescribe drugs, but many alternative specialists such as chiropractors and naturopaths use modern laboratory tests and equipment to help them diagnose symptoms. The multitherapeutic approach is also very effective in the treatment of menopausal symptoms.

But any approach a practitioner uses works best when it is personalized. You can save a great deal of time consulting with someone who is experienced and skilled in using alternatives. If, however, you are healthy, know your own body, and feel confident about doing your own research, there is no reason why *you* can't decide what vitamins and herbs to use—many other women do.

Herbs, vitamins, and homeopathic remedies are not "prescribed" the same way as drugs because they often do not work the same way on every body. Take herbs, for example.

To begin with, there are many different herbs for the same symptom, some that work more effectively on one person than another. Dosages also vary from individual to individual. This makes it difficult to recommend a standard herb that will work the same way for every woman. Practitioners fine-tune their recommendations for a specific body, and sometimes it takes experimentation to determine the most effective treatment. As you become more confident about using supplements—whether you consult with a specialist or not—you will also be more comfortable with the idea of trying different remedies and, once you find one that works for you, adjusting the dosages when necessary. The ability to know your body grows with practice.

Finding an Alternative Therapist

The diagnostic and treatment skills among the various therapists in the natural health field are more difficult to judge than are those among medical doctors, who share basically the *same* education and are more organized and supervised professionally. Many alternative practitioners are formally trained in colleges or special institutes. Chiropractors, acupuncturists, and some naturopaths are required to take state and/or national examinations in order to be licensed. But many others working in the alternative health field are self-taught or have served apprenticeships in different therapeutic approaches and possess considerable skill and knowledge. A number of them practice as private consultants and take clients only through referrals. (See "Healers," page 124.)

No single standard is recognized by all practitioners of

alternative medicine, although as the general field gains prominence and public acceptance, the licensed therapies are defining their standards more rigidly. Current attempts to restrict the practice of various disciplines affects members who use *many* alternative approaches even as it forces other nonmember practitioners to meet licensing standards. The nature and appeal of alternative medicine is diversity, and as consumers we need to have the broadest range of options—alternative and conventional.

The easiest way to find a practitioner you trust, with the background, knowledge, and experience you want, is through a personal recommendation. Many of us have found our gynecologists in this way. And I believe it is the *best* way. The great majority of alternative practitioners are credible and offer effective, responsible treatment. But irresponsible professionals exist in every field, and the way to avoid them is through firsthand information.

In large cities, finding a competent practitioners is not difficult, particularly in the West. Many alternative therapists practice in San Francisco, California; Portland, Oregon; Seattle, Washington; Santa Fe, New Mexico; and Boulder, Colorado. But the East Coast—always more conservative medically—is catching up fast. Talking with the manager of your local health food or vitamin outlet could be a convenient way to get into the natural health loop. The stores are often reliable centers for information, and their salespeople may be able to recommend a reliable practitioner. Many stores also hold clinics featuring prominent specialists or authors who discuss the uses of herbs and vitamins. Your local gym, fitness center, or exercise specialist may be able to recommend someone. Consult the resource list in the back of this book and look for the national organizations representing those alternative specializations that interest you most. They can help you locate a practitioner in your area.

To decide for yourself whether an alternative therapist is credible, use your critical powers, common sense, and intuition. Observe the healing environment. Is it clean? Is the staff respectful and pleasant? Do you feel comfortable with the therapist? People will tell you that it is naive to expect a rapport with your conventional medical doctor—skill, experience, and reputation are what counts. Certainly those qualities are important in all healing practices, but in alternative medicine, which treats the whole body and thus requires sensitivity and openness, compatibility is a real consideration. Does the diagnosis make sense? Does the treatment make you feel better? Will the practitioner answer your questions? Is she or he sensitive to your feelings and needs? Be suspicious of anyone in any discipline who practices mumbo-jumbo medicine. Effective alternative therapies are rational, and the people who practice them do not have secrets about what they do. They should be willing to tell you what they are doing and why they are doing it. They should demystify, not complicate the experience of healing. If what is said feels wrong to you, or doesn't make sense, speak up and don't be afraid to walk out.

The manner, style, and attitudes of alternative specialists—whether they are medical doctors or not—are often as different from each other as they are from conventional physicians. But the best alternative therapists and doctors I've met share some important qualities. They listen and observe well. They pay close attention to a client, and they know how to assess the physical, emotional, and psychological factors influencing the state of that person's health. They are able to make personalized recommendations for treatment of the whole body/mind, understanding that a problem or illness in one part of the body affects every part. No complaint is considered unimportant, and patients soon become aware that no symptom is too trivial to bring up. Good alternative therapists see their role as teachers who try to explain things simply. The doctor-patient relationship is a partnership, and in order for it to work, both patient and therapist feel free to express opinions and to ask questions without anxiety. Such a relationship empowers us as patients and tends to make us feel more responsible for doing what is necessary to stay healthy. Alternative therapies *need* the active involvement of the patient in the process of healing.

Patient responsibility in alternative medical treatment often extends to taking legal responsibility for care. Some therapists ask clients in advance to sign waivers absolving the practitioner for any side effects or negative outcomes resulting from treatment. (This is similar to the waiver medical doctors ask a patient to sign before using a new drug or treatment.)

Alternative practitioners often have independent suppliers for vitamins, herbs, and other supplements, which they dispense as part of their practice. Whenever a therapist dispenses supplements, you have the right and should take the responsibility to ask what the differences are between the private brands and those sold on the open market. Generally, the practitioner will explain that he or she believes the quality of the independent-brand supplements to be superior. Most likely the products have been formulated for easier absorption by the body and should thus work more effectively. However, the cost to you should be comparable to commercial brands sold in the health food store.

Most practitioners of alternative medicine are *against* the long-term use of any drug, including synthetic estrogen replacement therapy. They believe the risks of taking drugs even occasionally are serious, particularly so when they are prescribed for life, like estrogen.

However, taking advantage of advanced medical diagnostic techniques is not incompatible with using alternative treatments. Women can and should be aware of the things they can do to prevent illness. For example, it makes good common sense to practice regular breast self-examination, and most gynecologists recommend mammography once a year after age fifty. The amount of radiation in a single mammogram is probably not harmful, but discuss with your doctor the option of having yearly sonograms, which use sound waves, instead of mammograms. Recently, some comparative research has been done on the accuracy of sonograms versus mammograms,[3] and it was found that sonograms were far more accurate than mammograms, particularly in determining the presence of invasive cancers, cancers in lumpy or cystic breasts, and cysts.

Seeing a physician for regular check-ups is also a good idea, even if you prefer natural treatments. Doctors are resources; think about them that way. There are no guarantees when it comes to developing disease. Family history, unexpected or unknown exposure to radiation, environmental changes, and how our bodies react to mental or emotional stress can affect our health even if we take good care of ourselves. It is not a personal failure if you don't feel well or become ill while "doing everything right." But we can reduce the risk of developing disease and give ourselves every chance for recovery by using both natural and conventional means.

Menopause begins a series of physiological changes in our bodies—that is inevitable for all of us. But by going through a natural menopause, we learn to take care of our bodies, minds, and psyches so we can do the things we want to do, with the energy and enthusiasm we need to enjoy them. There are many approaches in alternative medicine, but all emphasize maintaining the health of the whole body, the whole person. Relieving the symptoms of menopause is an interim objective. Beyond that—once we learn to use natural remedies, treatments, and body/mind therapies—the benefits are life-enhancing forever. And there are no risks. With physical strength, mental resilience, and psychological wholeness, growing older becomes a journey we can look forward to with great expectations.

How to Use This Book

If this book is your introduction to alternative therapies, try to put aside any preconceived ideas you have about their use. Start from the beginning and resist the temptation to look first for the alternative solutions to your symptom or symptoms—they exist.

Read the interviews with the practitioners, find out how they work, how they think, and consider the range of possibilities they present for relief of symptoms, along with their professional opinions on the best way to maintain your health now and beyond menopause.

The interviews with the women who are currently managing their menopause naturally with programs that include supplements, diet, and exercise will show you how these therapies can work on a daily basis.

The last section offers more information on supplements and remedies. Included are the most common herbs for menopause, vitamins and minerals and cell salts to treat symptoms, and miscellaneous remedies collected from published sources to add to the information you will already have from the specialists and women interviewed.

The first step toward putting together your own health program is to read about the available alternatives to usual medical treatment and then begin with one approach that most immediately addresses your needs. Herbal medicine, vitamin therapy, homeopathy, and Chinese medicine all have treatments that will relieve menopausal symptoms. Reflexology, aromatherapy, and therapeutic massage are not primary treatments for these specific symptoms, although they all have value and can certainly be used to help alleviate symptoms, relax the body, enable it to balance itself. Self-hypnosis is a mind/body technique that, once learned, can help you deal with the stress and anxiety that often accompany physical symptoms. Many women combine different alternative methods to shape a program for themselves, but no program will be effective without paying attention to the food you eat. A nutritious and well-balanced diet is essential. You must also exercise—a combination of aerobic and weight resistance training—regardless of what other method(s) you select.

Choosing a system or discipline to follow will depend on your personal preferences, your affinity to the philosophical basis of the various treatments, and your willingness to become a partner in your health care.

Part Two

Alternative Approaches

The specialists I interviewed for this section were introduced to me by women who had consulted with them for menopausal symptoms or were looking for help with an exercise program or interested in body work. They are primarily women—only two men are included. It was not planned that way, but I have found, particularly in body work and massage, that more women seem to be practicing than men.

All but two are New York–based specialists. New York is not generally known for alternative medicine, but, in fact, the field is well represented in a city that has a remarkable population of medical doctors. I spoke with various therapists in other parts of the country, but phone interviews were somewhat unsatisfactory to me. I wanted to see the work environments of these practitioners, meet them, and, when possible, receive treatments as a patient or guidance as a student. This more personalized approach gave me a much clearer understanding of their philosophies and their treatment processes.

Some of these alternative therapies aim to relieve all menopausal symptoms and help prevent osteoporosis as well. Others treat each symptom separately. But by combining several therapies to improve your general health, and using herbs and/or vitamins to relieve any menopausal symptoms, developing a stronger body—and *not* whether or not you take estrogen—becomes the primary issue at menopause.

Alternative specialists who are medical doctors, homeopaths, or chiropractors often set up practices that mirror the healing environment and organizational routines of their conventional colleagues. Their offices are staffed with assistants and receptionists. Many have examining rooms and changing rooms. With a license to practice they can order the usual lab tests and X rays if necessary, and their treatments are covered by many insurance companies. They generally specialize in preventive medicine, are against invasive procedures, and recommend herbs and vitamins in preference to drugs. Some medical doctors are homeopaths, although all homeopaths are not medical doctors. It is important to remember when choosing an alternative practitioner that having a medical background is only one consideration among many. Weigh your judgments and make your decision based on what you need for your body and mind.

The Naturopathic Approach

Dr. Serafina Corsello, an M.D., became interested in holistic medicine in the early 1970s when, practicing conventional medicine, she became seriously concerned about the effects of using synthetic, often harsh chemicals on her patients. She began a determined exploration into many different natural approaches to healing—herbs, vitamins, minerals, diet, and exercise. The results she obtained with her patients through a multitherapeutic naturopathic approach strengthened her commitment to this mind/body direction in healing. Dr. Corsello became active in the American College of Advancement in Medicine, an organization that teaches chelation therapy. Chelation therapy is based on the intravenous administration of a synthetic amino acid that binds toxic substances and removes them from the system, primarily through the kidneys; in addition, the process removes calcium from the small arteries and deposits it in the bones. The result: a rejuvenation of cells and an aid in the reversal of osteoporosis. As a chelation therapist, Dr. Corsello has become one of the leaders in this field. She uses her knowledge of the cellular biochemistry of the body to treat her patients by predominantly natural means and specializes in natural alternatives for menopausal and perimenopausal symptoms.

Serafina Corsello, M.D.

The word *doctor* comes from the Latin *docere,* which means to teach, and I try to do just that by teaching my patients to stay healthy. I begin by looking at their eating habits and—particularly in menopausal women—I recommend they remove from their diets meat, alcohol, coffee, and other foods that tend to increase the acidity of the blood and leach calcium from the bones and exacerbate hot flashes. I recommend that women research nutritional supplementation thoroughly. Only through education can one take advantage of alternative medicine because knowledge is the power that makes change possible.

Once you understand that by balancing the chemistry of the cell, you can reverse pathological processes, it changes forever the way you see healing. The concept applies to anything from nervous disorders to gynecological disturbances. Many specific herbs and nutrients are capable of restoring the balance of different organs from the liver to the reproductive system. Most herbs have beneficial effects on the functions of specific organs while influencing the health of the whole body. The herb uva ursi, for example, works primarily on the urinary system but also helps with gynecological problems.

Over the past twenty years my challenge has been learning to interpret and differentiate what remedial substances to use for specific problems and for an effect on the total body. For instance, antioxidants are beneficial to all organs, but vitamin E in particular is essential to protect organs like the heart, brain, and liver. Vitamin E is a very important supplement for the treatment of menopausal symptoms.

Treating perimenopausal and menopausal symptoms naturally has become one of my main interests in the past ten years. It began with my own personal experience. I started hormone replacement therapy when I was fifty-two years old after entering menopause and suffering a serious case of insomnia and hot flashes. Both symptoms disappeared with the hormones, but I stopped taking them a few years later when I discovered a lump on my breast and feared cancer.

Although the results indicated that the mass was suspicious, I decided to forgo a biopsy and excision because I feared spreading a possible cancer lesion. I decided instead to try an alternative therapy and consulted with a doctor who had devised a nontoxic alternative—lipidic selenium and other minerals by injection and by mouth—combining his treatments with my own, which included loads of herbal remedies and antioxidants, chelation therapy, and almost daily vitamin C drips. But I still needed respite from my menopausal symptoms and began researching extensively.

I went to the library and took out as many books as I could on Chinese herbal remedies. I investigated the native American remedies and discovered there was a lot I could do myself, but I had to pick and choose from here and there. I was already taking calcium, magnesium, and lots of vitamins. I now needed herbal substances that would act like estrogen and progesterone, not only to restore my sleep, but to help me avoid the long-term consequences of hormone deprivation—osteoporosis and cardiovascular problems. I discovered dong quai, which is one of the oldest Chinese remedies for hot flashes. I also started taking ginseng in the morning, for both its estrogen-mimicking effect and its anticancer properties.

To cope with other menopausal symptoms, I began drinking anise and licorice tea to relieve fatigue and to restore cortical adrenal functions. I also took gamma amino butyric acid (GABA), an amino-acid-and-vitamin combination that calms the brain, especially at night. I also took the calcium and magnesium at night, not only to help me sleep better, but to strengthen my bones and cardiovascular system. I added the trace mineral boron to my regimen. Boron helps increase the estrogen activity as well as the uptake of calcium by the bones. I took large amounts of vitamin E—400 IU in the morning and 1200 IU with the evening meal. And I took all of these substances together to avoid the hormonal storm that comes when you stop using estrogen and progesterone abruptly, as I did. I found that my menopausal symptoms cleared up within a few days. And a year later X rays revealed no traces of a mass in my breast.

Whether one prefers synthetic hormone replacement or an alternative mode, most women want to help themselves in some way when they reach menopause. Statistics show that only 15 percent of menopausal women are symptom free, and these are women who have high levels of stored estrogen in their fatty tissues. The majority of the rest of the women have mild to moderate problems.

The cortex of the adrenal gland produces three different kinds of hormones. The most important in menopause is dehydroepiandrosterone (DHEA); it is DHEA produced by the adrenals that is transformed into estrogen and acts as the "backup system" in our bodies to give us hormone support after "ovarian failure." But the aging process, allergies, and high levels of stress deplete the adrenal glands of hormones, so most women enter menopause with very low DHEA. Any endocrine gland that is overused loses its capacity to produce adequate amounts of hormones. As I often say when I lecture, "When one uses it and abuses it, one loses it." Stress depletes the body not only of DHEA, but of the vitamins and minerals necessary to metabolize hormones into their active form. The most important nutrients commonly lost are B_6, zinc, and magnesium, which are excreted during chronic illnesses, the aging process, overactivity, and stress. If one understands what is necessary for proper metabolic function during menopause, one can compensate for what is being lost and, by doing so, restore the natural balance of nature.

The period before ovarian hormonal production stops completely is called *perimenopause.* During this stage, menopausal symptoms are always worse. In some women perimenopause can last from five to ten years and can begin as early as the mid-thirties. During the latter stages all symptoms can become more intense. The abrupt peaks and valleys of erratic estrogen and progesterone production create a roller coaster of symptoms and emotions. Some of the symptoms include a change in mood and attention span, subtle changes in sleep patterns, and a mild intolerance to heat. By using multiple natural interventions, as I did, one can relieve these symptoms.

When the symptoms occur, one can increase magnesium in the morning and calcium at night; vitamin E, dong quai, and ginseng counteract these symptoms efficiently, as I myself confirmed.

Also progesterone—the hormone necessary to keep us from aborting (or having a miscarriage)—can transform itself into DHEA and estrogen needed by the body during perimenopause and menopause. Instead of synthetic progesterone, I prefer using natural forms of progesterone such as the one from the wild Mexican yam contained in Progest Cream (see page 31), orginally formulated as a night cream for menopausal women. Unlike synthetic progesterone, it does not produce side effects. Progest is a proprietary name for a progesterone cream that I have used since it first came out. I recommend massaging it directly on the skin. (See page 31 for directions on how to use Progest Cream.) A significant additional benefit is that it does reverse the acceleration of the skin's aging process.

Most women need progesterone even before they stop menstruating because we take in added estrogen from beef, milk, chicken, and the eggs we eat. Animal feed is supplemented regularly with estrogen, but not with progesterone.

This natural approach to menopause is preferred not only by me, but by 90 percent of my patients. They come to me asking for safe alternatives. Ten percent of my patients choose hormone replacement therapy, but even for them, adding minerals and nutrients to their personal programs and paying attention to their diets is extremely beneficial. Not only does this help them maintain a youthful appearance, but I believe it helps to diminish the chances of developing cancers associated with pharmaceutical hormone replacement therapy.

The appropriate supplementation depends on the individual patient, but it always includes vitamin E and other antioxidants—those vitamins, minerals, and enzymes that can help protect our bodies from free radicals—the unbalanced molecular structures that cause disease by impairing our immune system. Calcium, magnesium, boron, zinc, vitamins A and K, and copper are also essential for proper bone nutrition. Vitamin C improves the strength and health of collagen—the gelatinous substance found in bones and cartilage as well as in many different tissues.

While in the latter stages of menopause one needs extra amounts of herbs, vitamins, and minerals, all my patients have been able to reduce the amounts as well as the number of different substances they take once they are stabilized. For instance, I now do not need to take dong quai every day, but as soon as I have any sensation of warmth or discomfort, I return to my usual dosages for a week to ten days. When I am working hard under stress, I need to take my remedies regularly. But I never stop taking vitamin E, calcium, magnesium, boron, and the antioxidants. And I now use progesterone cream on my neck, face, and breasts every other night.

During menopause hormone imbalances cause some women to gain a great deal of weight due to a "diabeticlike" condition called *insulin resistance.* This state occurs when insulin will not bind properly to the tissues, causing carbohydrates to be stored as fatty deposits instead of entering the cells to be burned as energy. To help prevent this condition, women must exercise, learn to relax, and eat low-carbohydrate diets rich in fiber. Proper nutrient intake is vital to maintaining the body's cellular balance and to helping diminish the symptoms of menopause.

Women also need to pay special attention to the quality and quantities of the foods they consume during menopause. Foods that are rich in carbohydrates—especially simple sugars—tend to increase hot flashes. Also any food that increases the acidity of the blood tends to leach calcium out of the bones and can promote osteoporosis. Blood acidifiers include coffee, tea, alcohol, meats, and sodas. High in phosphorous, they displace calcium from the bones. Of course, smoking and uncontrolled stress also raise blood acidity.

Osteoporosis is a condition that can develop in the body when hormone production ends and the bones become demineralized, softer, and thinner. Osteoporosis causes the spine to shrink and women to become shorter and bent. Women at risk are those with a family history of the condition—many are from Nordic/European extraction and are fair, thin, and tall.

In a recent study *The New England Journal of Medicine* concluded that a proper balance of progesterone is more important than estrogen for healthy bones. While estrogen limits the breakdown of bones, progesterone increases bone rebuilding. Dr. John Lee (see page 205) and other researchers discovered that women who used a natural progesterone cream had little or no incidence of osteoporosis.

Stretching of the body during yoga or low-impact aerobics is also extremely helpful in making certain that the minerals get attached to the bone cells—the osteoclasts.

I have formulated a bone-protecting supplement for my patients that contains boron—a micromineral, used in very small quantities. The medical literature recommends 12 mg of boron a day, but in this formula 4 mg is sufficient in combination with all the other nutrients I have included. Boron makes the estrogen a woman has in her body work more efficiently. In addition to boron, this supplement contains vitamin D to increase the bonding of calcium to the bone, silica to increase its strength, and various forms of calcium to assure its absorption, including the best form for bone rebuilding—microcrystalline hydroxyapatite. A small amount of phosphorous is also included for the formation of calcium triphosphate, the mineral formation component of bones.

The amount of calcium needed to avoid osteoporosis

and what kind of calcium to take are both debatable issues. The decisions depend on the needs of an individual woman's body and her life-style. Anyone who tells you that all you have to do to have healthy bones is take 1500 to 2000 mg of calcium a day does not understand bone metabolism. For example, women who eat beef or drink sodas regularly may require a higher calcium intake than women who don't because phosphorous-containing foods remove calcium from the bones. The best forms of calcium are microcrystalline hydroxyapatite, calcium citrate, and calcium carbonate, though people who have low gastric acidity, for instance, cannot absorb calcium carbonate. These products are all available over-the-counter at your vitamin store.

Tofu is a protein component of soy beans and is known to have vital estrogen properties. Strange as it may seem, its estrogenic properties are closer to our natural estrogen than the estrogen of the pregnant mare used in Premarin. Tofu is a very versatile food—basically tasteless—and when combined with other foods assumes their flavors. Tofu is also easy to digest and extremely pleasant when prepared properly. I only buy organic tofu made naturally—some commercial brands are made by combining the soy protein with chemicals and should be avoided. Chemical ingredients tend to bind with hormones, creating toxic by-products that can be damaging to the liver and much of the rest of the body, making menopausal symptoms worse.

Ginseng is a great herbal remedy. I recommend the Chinese form from the Jilen mountains, which has the highest concentration of ginsemite—the active ingredient. Ginseng is an adaptogen, which means it has the ability to improve the general functioning of cells, and it is also a DNA and cell membrane stabilizer. Consequently ginseng is anticarcinogenic. Ginseng also has estrogenlike qualities and helps in the management of hot flashes without the cancer-inducing risk of pharmaceutical estrogen.

I can't stress enough the importance of vitamin E in a program for menopause. It, too, has estrogenlike properties and being an antioxidant protects the hormones from damage. If a hormone is damaged in its structure, it not only stops doing the job it is delegated to do, but actually becomes a carcinogenic substance.

As most people age their bodies lose the ability to break down oily vitamins like E and process them into water-soluble vitamins that can be used by the body. This process is called *micellization.* For that reason I often recommend an already micellized form of vitamin E for my patients.

The newest arrival in the field of estrogen replacement therapy is a natural estrogen cream from natural vegetable sources. This cream contains 80 percent estriol, the protective estrogen hormone that is excreted primarily during pregnancy. European studies show that this is the hormone that protects women against the carcinogenic effect of estradiol—the most common form of estrogen. The cream contains only 10 percent estriol and 10 percent estrone. I often like to mimic the natural cycle by using fifteen days of natural estrogen cream and fifteen days of natural progesterone cream. Only women who have serious vaginal dryness need to use this as a vaginal cream. Most women do very well with natural progesterone cream. This, in conjunction with all the other things that I have recommended, proves to be very beneficial. Since progesterone ultimately becomes estrogen, I keep women on natural estrogen cream only for six months to a year, depending on the severity of their menopausal symptoms. The dosage of estrogen in the cream is ten times less than that of Premarin, but it's much more efficient since the potency of natural estrogen cream is similar to our own estrogen.

As you can see, much can be done to restore proper hormonal balance and to avoid the consequences of unmanaged menopause. But in addition to herbs and supplements, women need to learn how to manage their stress if they want to control menopausal symptoms effectively. My recommendations are aimed at bringing back the wisdom of nature.

Dr. Corsello's Program for Healthy Older Women

This basic treatment program is excerpted from my patient literature handout and is based on the use of natural treatments for perimenopausal and menopausal symptoms. Most of these substances are available at health food stores.

Progest Cream

If still menstruating, you can massage 1 tsp. of cream from day #14 to onset of period on breast, neck, face, or elsewhere. If periods have become irregular or have stopped, massage ½ tsp. of the cream twice a day, every other day, into skin. For more information on Progest Cream, call 1-800-866-9085.

Dong Quai

200 mg in capsule form, 3 times a day.

Ginseng

2 capsules, powdered, preferably before breakfast and before lunch; ginseng may cause sleep disruptions if taken late at night.

Menopautonic (a liquid herbal supplement by Naturae Medica, Santa Fe, New Mexico)

This supplement combines dong quai, black cohosh, licorice, and other herbs that restore gynecological balance and help greatly to relieve hot flashes. Dosage needs to be tailored to individual needs, but an average dose is 40 drops twice a day. If symptoms do not disappear, increase drops until the hot flashes cease. If warmed by hot flashes at night, take more at bedtime.

Vitamin E

2 doses a day: 400 IU of mixed tocopherol with breakfast and 800–1200 IU with dinner. If using micellized vitamin E (see page 215), take only one-third of the dosage of mixed tocopherol.

Boron

4 to 12 mg a day. Use 12 mg if taken alone, less if taken with my supplement.

Licorice

300 mg 3 times a day. If used in combination, see "Menopautonic."

Calcium

A combination formulated with 1500 mg of calcium, 400 IU of vitamin D, 2–4 mg of boron, and the other micronutrients necessary for proper bone metabolism.

Chiropractic

There is no question that as alternative medicine gains greater visibility, chiropractic doctors, particularly those whose work takes them beyond spinal adjustment, are beginning to take on greater professional stature. Many insurance companies now cover chiropractic treatment. Dr. Loretta Mears and Dr. Neil Kobetz are two such specialists. To become chiropractic physicians they and their colleagues were required to take the same premed school courses as the conventional medical student—biochemistry, general chemistry, organic chemistry, biology, physics, anatomy, and so on, in addition to the social sciences—as part of their degree program in chiropractic. Because they are conventionally educated in the sciences, unlike many other alternative practitioners, chiropractors understand the human body and how it works. However, these unique health care providers also have the freedom to explore alternate forms of healing and use that knowledge within their eclectic practices, as do allopathic doctors, who extend their practice of medicine to include alternative therapies and treatments. There are thirteen chiropractic colleges in the United States and Canada.

Conventional medicine had tended to dismiss the theory of chiropractics developed by Daniel Palmer (1845–

1913) until his son Bartlett Joshua continued Palmer's work. He was in today's terms a marketing expert who lobbied chiropractic successfully through state legislatures and secured legal licensing for the profession. But veterbral adjustment as a technique to cure all disease was by no means accepted unilaterally. Willard Carver believed that nutrition, physical therapy, and herb and vitamin counseling were equally essential, so he split off from the Palmers. His followers were known as the "mixers," and the practice they advocated is predominant today, although there are "straights" who focus on vertebral realignment.

Andrew Weil, M.D., in his fascinating book *Health and Healing,* says this about chiropractic: "[Vertebral adjustment] . . . can be a valuable addition to a doctor's therapeutic repertory, both because it involves a laying-on of hands that can foster productive relationships with patients and because it may improve the circulation of blood and nervous energy to ailing parts of the body. . . . Yoga and other Oriental systems of mind-body development assign highest importance to the spine as the conduit of basic life energy from 'out there' to 'in here.' "

In the treatment of menopausal changes Dr. Kobetz and Dr. Mears and other chiropractors who combine a variety of alternative treatments—according to women who have consulted with them—have been very successful in diminishing uncomfortable symptoms, relieving stress, and rebalancing the body.

Although Dr. Loretta Mears is known professionally as a chiropractor, she regards herself as a primary care physician. Neither designation fully describes her holistic approach to health care nor reflects her wisdom on the subject of women and aging. Correcting vertebral misalignments and practicing kinesiology are only two of the tools she employs to bring her patients to health. Trained in herbal medicine and nutrition before becoming a chiropractor, she is comfortable combining conventional and unconventional diagnostic methods and treatments as necessary and appropriate to aid healing physical conditions without using drugs. Dr. Mears says, "My grandmother made herbal tonics every spring to clear the blood. Natural remedies were a valued part of my black heritage."

Loretta Mears, D.C.

I see the time of menopause as a natural opportunity for women to make substantive emotional and psychological changes in their lives while their bodies are undergoing dramatic physical ones. I think women need to realize that these years—the middle ones and the years of growing older—are a time to reestablish attention not only on ourselves, but on the women we care about—our sisters, our cousins, our friends, our mothers, and our grandmothers if they're still around. We have information and support to give each other. Female knowledge has too long been dismissed as being insignificant.

Many women are anxious and unfocused when they think about menopause and growing older. They feel they've lost their value in the culture and in their families. In fact, this can be a great opportunity to focus on our own value as individuals.

It may be a time to take up yoga or t'ai chi or to begin taking a class that focuses on some talent that needs to be developed. Or to get counseling for some personal issues that need to be confronted. Rather than suggest that menopause makes women crazy (as in popular mythology), I see the "change" as a great opportunity to explore our relationships with ourselves and those close to us because of the heightened mind/body awareness many women experience.

The metaphor of a garden can speak to women very clearly. A garden that's newly dug needs to be prepared for the work it will do. There isn't much reward right away. It's only later that you get the raspberries and asparagus. Lots of plants take many years to mature, but most people don't grow them because they want to see the bounty right away. If we begin to realize that all our life's experience has given us a fertility—a foundation that everyone we know can benefit from—then we would use what we know more confidently.

If a woman has menopausal symptoms and comes to me, I take a very thorough case history. In addition to a medical history I feel it is equally important to have in-depth life-style information—the nature of the work someone does, how leisure time is spent, diet, type of exercise, sleep patterns—because the way a woman lives her life is part of her health profile. My initial visits can last about an hour and a half. I then do a physical examination as well as an orthopedic and neurological examination and a chiropractic assessment of the patient. I use these examinations to help me determine where problems might lie and if the health care I offer is the best treatment at this time. Some people may also require laboratory tests or X rays.

If the diagnostic process suggests that a team approach is necessary, I often help a patient coordinate the various treatments. I refer to acupuncturists, homeopaths, massage therapists, internists, neurologists, and so on.

In addition to the information that examinations give me about a person's heart, lungs, digestive, nervous, and musculoskeletal systems, they also help me understand how a woman lives in or with her body, her pain response, and the places she holds pain, tension, and fear. I believe we all hold the challenges and successes of our lives in our bodies.

Most of the people I see have health crises because of chronic problems that have gone untreated. Women are especially prone to denying the severity of their pain or symptoms until it is unbearable or someone pushes them to seek treatment. But sometimes making simple changes like a new mattress, or holding the telephone differently, or adjusting the height of a keyboard, or replacing worn-out shoes helps balance the body. Usually chiropractic manipulation and immediate ergonomic changes can give enough relief so we can then move to work on deeper levels if the patient desires. At this point we would begin a nutritional assessment, which could result in recommendations for vitamin supplementation, changes in eating habits, or herbal remedies for ongoing problems.

The signs of menopause—hot flashes, mood swings, depression, night sweats, and irregular periods—can be diminished by a variety of alternative therapies, but a woman has to be willing to experiment. I think that's one of the most important lessons of menopause. Each woman is different, and her hormonal changes vary so much from day to day and month to month, that it would be impractical to monitor the daily changes as they occur. What I try to do is work on an overall level to improve the quality of life. It means experimenting with different herbs, with different body-work techniques, different meditation exercises.

Many of us believe any treatment should yield immediate results or be dismissed as ineffective. We've come to expect a "magic potion" that will cure all our distress or other symptoms right away. This is a Western cultural bias because, in truth, the body does not heal instantly, and holistic or alternative therapies—which gently support the body in its healing process—take more time than most of us are willing to allow. They do not force the body to heal. Most alternative therapies can take days or weeks to eliminate the symptoms of a health crisis because they work on changing the underlying conditions causing the crisis.

When hormone levels change, not only are your uterus and ovaries affected—your temperature regulating system, your muscle tone, your bones, and your digestion and mood are also affected. But it's important for women to know hormone changes take place in women's bodies throughout their lives, not only at menopause. The changes are vastly different in different women. The hormones that fluctuate up and down during menopause are the same ones that cause mood swings when you have PMS. Hormone changes are a fact of life in every woman's body.

One of the difficult issues in alternative medicine is that the practitioner can't do the work of healing without the patient sharing some of the responsibility for getting better. Many of my patients are reluctant to take an active part in their health care, expecting that health is given to us with little investment of our own time or energy. They ask, "Isn't there a pill or some drops I can take?" Herbal suppliers and health food stores and many alternative health care practitioners encourage us to use herbal and homeopathic remedies as substitutes for more dangerous pharmaceutical drugs. Herbs were never meant to be a substitute for drugs. Herbs are a support to be used in a total life plan that encourages health and well-being. There is no magic herb to substitute for regular exercise or a balanced nutritional program.

Pursuing alternative medicine is not a static exploration. People find the practitioner they need when they learn more about their bodies, become more aware of their different emotional needs. That knowledge and awareness may mean changing practitioners to find one who is able to understand what you need.

Herbs have been used for centuries by women to help with menopausal signs. Heavy and/or irregular bleeding (menorrhagia) may be helped by using herbs with natural bioflavonoids. Some fruits and herbs like red clover and bilberry may also be helpful for flooding.

Oatstraw, cayenne pepper, blessed thistle, ginger, black cohosh, blue cohosh, wild yam root, false unicorn root, fennel, passion flower, peppermint, hops, chamomile, kelp, and alfalfa are just a few of the herbs I've used for dealing with the signs of hot flashes, depression, fatigue, and insomnia.

Herbs selected with the individual's needs in mind and used in moderation with the guidance of a knowledgeable herbalist can be extremely useful at menopause. Herbs may take longer to work than pharmaceutical drugs, but they are less toxic when used properly.

Vitamin E can be very helpful for some women. I recommend 800–1000 IU daily. It has helped up to 70 percent of women in some studies with skin dryness, hot flashes, and mood swings and can also be applied internally for vaginal dryness. One recommended regimen suggests daily internal application of the contents of one capsule—prick a capsule, squeeze the liquid on your finger, and apply—for four to six weeks and then once weekly to maintain the benefits. Each woman will have to experiment to find her level of maximum benefit.

I have found daily supplementation with bioflavonoids—to strengthen capillaries—like vitamin C, calcium citrate, beta-carotene (the vegetable precursor to vitamin A), and possibly zinc citrate and the B-complex to be helpful in maintaining overall health during menopause. Each woman should establish her daily program with the help of her health care providers.

Normally, at age forty both women and men begin to lose .5 percent of bone/skeleton every year. After menopause the rate increases to 1–2 percent a year. By age sixty a woman can have lost 40 percent of her skeleton and is at risk for developing osteoporosis from calcium loss. It need not be due to dietary insufficiency of the mineral. One must not lose more calcium in feces, urine, and sweat than is taken in through food to maintain a positive calcium balance. A nutritional program that is more than 30 percent protein increases calcium excretion because metabolism of the protein acidifies the body, which then tries to achieve its normal alkaline balance by excreting calcium. We can help intestinal absorption of calcium by getting enough vitamin D (thirty minutes' exposure to the sun three times a week on the face and hands—it need not be direct sun—should be enough for the body to make the vitamin D required). Boron, a mineral necessary for calcium metabolism, rarely needs to be supplemented because the small amount we require is present in fruits, vegetables, and nuts.

The risk factors for osteoporosis are well known: low calcium intake over a lifetime, smoking, too much dietary protein (animal products), daily cortisone use, antacids containing aluminum, or the removal of both ovaries prior to menopause. Small-framed women who have less dense bone structure are also more at risk for osteoporosis—Northern European white women and Asian women, for example.

Vegan vegetarians—those who don't eat any animal protein: no meat, fish, eggs, or dairy products—have higher bone density than the general population. Vegetarians have alkaline body chemistry and hold more calcium. The Chinese, for example, have higher bone density than the Japanese because the Japanese diet is higher in animal protein.

A nutritional program based on a variety of vegetables, fruits, nuts, grains, and beans and low in fat and animal protein and dairy products is especially helpful during menopause. Such a dietary plan not only maximizes the body's positive calcium balance and therefore prevents osteoporosis, but may also prevent breast, colon, ovarian, and uterine cancers and other degenerative ailments.

Daily exercise is critical for health and to maintain strong muscles and bones. And any weight-bearing exercise helps prevent bone loss. Sustained physical work, light lower- and upper-body weight training for a minimum of twenty minutes, should be done three times a week.

I believe that body work of many types—shiatsu, massage, reflexology, and so forth—can help ease a woman's transition through menopause. All of them offer different benefits, but common to each are increased circulation, relaxation, and touch—the laying on of hands. Caring touch is healing to humans because we are touch-sensitive animals. I encourage my patients to read about and try different bodywork techniques as support for the ongoing chiropractic care they receive.

I don't talk about "symptoms" when discussing menopause, I talk about signs and changes. Symptoms indicate a degenerative or pathological process, and normal menopause is not pathological. Hot flashes, precipitous mood swings, headaches, back pain, menstrual flooding, vaginal dryness, hair loss, short-term memory loss, depression, and insomnia can all occur with menopause and cause minimal discomfort or major distress. But each woman is different, and many have few or no signs of menopause. The signs are a normal part of growing older and can last for a few weeks, several months, or years. Women who have hot flashes, insomnia, or backaches are not necessarily sick. If, at some point in the change, your signs are severe, talk to other women about what they've done, explore herbs, supplement your regular diet with vitamins, exercise regularly, and find a homeopath, chiropractor, or naturopath you can trust to listen and respond to your needs.

If a woman never allows time to evaluate her menopause—sometimes risking discomfort—she may opt to use drugs before she knows whether she needs them. I believe that only one-third or less of the women who are currently receiving hormones actually need them. Women are often unaware that the usual prescription is to take HRT for the rest of their lives. One less drastic option is to use hormones just as a support over the period of time when the signs of menopause are most uncomfortable. Women will continue to have light menstrual periods for as long as they stay on hormones.

It is a normal, natural change for women to stop menstruating. Aging, too, is natural, and we can make it a healthy process. I think most women feel that the risks of HRT outweigh the possible discomfort of menopausal signs, but women must be willing to take some responsibility for monitoring and maintaining their health.

When we ignore the more gentle signs our bodies offer to tell us of misuse or overindulgence—like colds, flu, and headaches—we set the stage for the development of chronic and possibly degenerative illness.

Health is a dynamic process. The body is constantly tearing down and rebuilding itself, and a careful balance between that destruction and repair is the area where we claim good health. But there is no such thing as a permanent state of good health. Periodic illness and discomfort are natural changes and are part of the body's natural process.

I believe menopause is a time for growth, experimentation, and a time for challenging what society tells us it means to be a healthy, whole woman.

Applied Kinesiology

Dr. Neil Kobetz is a chiropractic physician who specializes in applied kinesiology—evaluating normal and abnormal body function by the use of muscle tests. Kinesiology is practiced by only about 2 percent of all chiropractors. A former physical education teacher, Kobetz further pursued his interest in body conditioning and fitness at the New York Chiropractic College, where in 1984 he received his doctorate in chiropracty.

Dr. Kobetz says that most chiropractic therapy involves treating basically healthy people who want to prevent serious illness. "I think that the techniques we use in chiropractic like applied kinesiology, nutrition, and homeopathic remedies are among the best ways to help people. We want our patients to enjoy optimal health and prevent them from going into a diseased state. Patients should feel energized and energetic. They don't have to have hot flashes in menopause. They can feel great all the time."

Neil Kobetz, D.C.

Chiropractic adjusts the spine, moves the vertebrae—and it is done noninvasively without surgical procedures. Its purpose is to allow proper nerve flow to a particular organ, gland, or muscle in the body. There are a number of ways to perform all the adjustments very gently despite the talk you may hear about cracking and snapping necks and heads.

In addition to traditional chiropractic adjustments, other therapies are also used to determine the state of a person's health and to bring a patient back to normal.

We do blood analysis. We work with nutritional programs to encourage general health. We work on certain reflex points in the body—neurolymphatic and neurovascular—with touch. "Neuro" is nerve-related; "lymphatic" refers to the lymph system, which carries body waste products. To find those points, we use applied kinesiology to test the neurological hookup of muscles with their corresponding organs and glands. If we determine that the muscle is fatigued, we test different areas to find out what will strengthen that muscle and how it is related to the part of the body that needs attention.

When patients come to me, I generally tell them that they should see a change in five to seven visits. These treatments occur at a frequency of one to two times a week for about three weeks. If nothing happens, then I'm not on the right track, and the patient may need a different method to make the correction.

If a woman has menopausal symptoms—hot flashes, night sweats—there is fatigue in the body. Not enough estrogen or too much estrogen, an imbalance between the estrogen/progesterone levels. I try to normalize the system so that a woman is getting proper energy flowing to the areas that need it most. It could be the reproductive organs or an organ like the liver. Maybe it's in the endocrine system—the pituitary, thyroid, or adrenal glands. In essence we try first to discover the fatigued areas through kinesiology, then we work to balance them. We might use vitamin E or bioflavonoids. Adrenal or homeopathic support or other natural supplements and remedies might be necessary. Kinesiology can test a nutritional supplement on a woman's body and tell us whether it will help her or not. We place a supplement in the patient's mouth, and depending on the muscle response obtained—when, for example, the patient's extended arm or leg is pressed—we analyze the movement to determine whether her system is reacting positively or negatively to the supplement.

Women should remember that not everything works on every body. The problem with prescribing for oneself is that over-the-counter nutritional supplements may not be formulated in the right combination(s), or perhaps the dosages are too high or not high enough. With kinesiology we can be more specific. Once you understand what you need, you're treating yourself with a greater understanding of how things work. The primary thing I try to do in the office is educate. Once you know what works for you, getting recommendations from friends is fine. But remember: every body is different. Experimenting works sometimes, but in general, the more specific the testing, the better the results.

Bioflavonoids, vitamin E, pantothenic acid (B_5), PABA, raw adrenal concentrate, or ginseng frequently work to diminish hot flashes and night sweats. Whatever you take for night sweats should help insomnia when both occur. Most women wake up because of the flush. Chamomile tea or passion flower or valerian root helps insomniacs and may also work well for menopausal women.

A hormonal imbalance or general body fatigue can cause fuzzy-headedness or memory loss—a complaint of menopause. Some studies show that certain nutritional supplements are beneficial for memory: inositol and choline or the herb ginkgo biloba extract.

I recommend calcium to all women. In the last five or six years a different type of calcium has come on the market—microcrystalline-hydroxyapatite, or MCHC, a calcium apatite with boron, which helps the body to absorb the calcium. MCHC seems to prevent the bone loss or bone demineralization that leads to osteoporosis. The studies seem to show that the benefits of MCHC outperform all other forms of calcium, including calcium lactate, citrate, carbonate, gluconate, and oyster-shell calcium.

I recommend following the label directions as they appear on the bottle. Don't overdose on any nutritional supplement.

Exercise is extremely important. Exercise strengthens the whole system. You rid the body of toxins, support the cardiovascular system, improve circulation. I think doing aerobics is excellent. Many of my patients are using the StairMaster or working out on the NordicTrack. Personally I'm not a major fan of an exercise bike because it's too fatiguing for the lower back and disk system.

Yoga, which is not cardiovascular, works very well for some people. Right now I've recommended yoga as therapy for a patient to strengthen a particular area of her body. Even exercise has to be personalized because of specific individual needs.

I emphasize good nutrition as part of any complete program for women as they grow older, but I'm not partial to a vegetarian diet. I think it's a little too restricting over the long haul. I think it can be beneficial to the system in short spurts—possibly a month or so at a time. Chicken fish, vegetables, rice—all fine. I'd suggest cutting down on the red meat, fats, spices, alcohol, drugs. Refined carbohydrates should be limited, but I don't think people need to restrict themselves obsessively. A cup of coffee each day isn't going to tire the system. If it does, that person has a lot more problems than coffee.

In general, I instruct every one of my patients to drink more water than they normally do. Most people don't know when to drink water or how much water to drink. I usually guide them according to body weight—most need about ten to twelve glasses of water a day, in addition to drinking other liquids—teas, juices, and so on. I suggest only five or six ounces of water every hour for the first ten to twelve hours of the working day. It oxygenates the system, flushes out toxins, dilutes stomach acids, and supports the muscles.

Twelve ounces of water at any one time is usually too much for the system—it's overloading. Don't drink water or fluids while you are eating—it tires your intestines. I can't stress enough the importance of supporting your system with small amounts of water during the day. Every chemical and enzymatic reaction in the body requires water. Without it your body goes into chemical stress—enough stress can affect other chemicals in your body.

As a woman ages she needs different types of programs at each stage, and you have to monitor these accordingly. Menopause occurs for different lengths of time in every woman. Someone may need more protein or less protein, more or less nutritional support—vitamins, herbs, diet changes. The only thing that remains constant is exercise, which should be basically the same at every age from menopause on.

Homeopathy

Homeopathy is a system of medicine developed in the early part of the nineteenth century by Samuel Hahnemann. According to Dr. Rebecca Elmaleh, a homeopathic medical doctor, homeopathic treatment makes use of a "microdose of a natural substance—usually plant, mineral, or animal—which if taken in full strength (a toxic dosage) would produce symptoms similar to those the patient is experiencing. This microdose relieves the symptoms and stimulates the body to achieve balance."

Despite the fact that no clinical trials or studies have been conducted, a growing number of advocates claim relief from conditions that range from menopausal symptoms to serious mental disturbances like psychosis.[4]

The effectiveness of the remedies depends on the skill of the practitioner. Self-medication is possible—to obtain many of the remedies does not require a medical prescription—but in-depth knowledge of the range of remedies used to treat a specific condition is necessary, as well as the patience to experiment. Dr. Elmaleh, along with other strict homeopaths, believes that homeopathy works best under the guidance of a specialist. Few homeopaths are willing to offer even general indications of remedies or dosages. The remedies must be individualized to a specific patient for maximum effectiveness.

A graduate of the University of Maryland Medical School, Dr. Elmaleh completed her residency in 1985 in family practice at Montefiore Medical Center in the Bronx, where she was chief resident. Her interest in homeopathy began during the next six years, when she headed a nonprofit community health center. She discovered that by combining allopathic and homeopathic approaches to medicine, she could provide a broader scope of health care for her patients.

Rebecca Elmaleh, M.D.

There are no licensed training programs for homeopathy in this country, but many courses are available—seminars, conferences, lectures—so I studied for three years here and then in France, where there are more facilities for homeopathic training. I consider myself a physician who has specialized in homeopathic medicine.

Homeopathic remedies are most commonly prepared in the form of small sugar pellets to be dissolved under the tongue. Let me give you a concrete example of how homeopathic remedies work: Ipecac is a syrup made from a South American plant. Full-strength ipecac is used to induce vomiting immediately. Most family households have ipecac in their medicine cabinets in case you need to induce vomiting because a child has inadvertently swallowed a poisonous substance. But the homeopathic preparation of ipecac given in a very, very diluted form is used when you don't want to induce vomiting, when you want instead to stop it. Homeopathic ipecac will cure the vomiting and other physical reactions that accompany it no matter what the reason—pregnancy, a cold, indigestion, and so forth. When the microdose of ipecac is taken, the physical response is exactly opposite from the reaction to taking it full strength. That's the basis of homeopathy. It is a completely individualized practice. We focus in on the patient as a unique person with a unique set of symptoms, and we look at those symptoms in the context of who the patient is, physically and emotionally, without regard for a diagnosis. When a practitioner matches a patient's symptoms to one remedy or several remedies, the symptoms end, resulting in a cure.

I can't emphasize enough that in homeopathy we do not diagnose. That's why it is standard procedure in my office to request that patients come to me with their medical records, reports on blood tests, and full evaluations of their condition, along with the recommendations of their regular doctors. This gives me the background information I need to understand what I am dealing with. Once I am clear that the condition a patient has is not life-threatening, I can proceed to treat the symptoms homeopathically to effect a cure. But I was trained as a physician to make a medical diagnosis, so if I determine a patient needs to be treated with conventional medicine, I refer her immediately to specialists for evaluation and testing. I don't treat such cases homeopathically.

What homeopathic treatment does is stimulate the immune system and trigger the body's natural defense mechanism so the body understands what it needs to do to cure itself. Ultimately, healing happens from within the body. Homeopathy deals directly with symptoms, never covering them up the way many drugs do.

There are over three thousand remedies in the homeopathic lexicon. These are used mostly to treat chronic illnesses not easily dealt with by conventional means. Chronic illnesses are seldom considered to be "medically life-threatening" but are devastating to the patients. Asthma, allergies, PMS, vaginitis, ear infections, arthritis, and, of course, menopausal symptoms respond to homeopathic treatment.

Hot flashes, fatigue, depression and disorientation, headaches—all symptoms of menopause—can be handled easily with homeopathy, but the same remedies do not work the same way on all women, so there is no such thing in homeopathy as a "hot flash remedy," although there are a range of remedies often used to treat the symptoms of menopause.

Homeopaths regard menopause as the time in a woman's life—because of hormonal changes—when she may experience unusual symptoms, both emotional and physical. I've discovered over time that some of the most bizarre symptoms can be menopause related. By the time women come to me with these symptoms, they have often been tested conventionally with negative results. One woman was tested with both CAT scans and an MRI! She came to me with burning pains that began on her face. They moved to her upper extremities and then to her lower extremities. She couldn't sleep or function. Her physician was very concerned and rightly so. Could it have been a serious disease like multiple sclerosis? No one knew. She went from neurologist to neurologist, and no one could explain the pains. I treated the symptoms with homeopathic remedies, and in a couple of weeks they disappeared. Once the pain was gone, however, the hot flashes came back, which we then treated.

We see this process occuring in homeopathy all the time. The body replaces one set of symptoms for another, and we continue curing each symptom until the body is balanced. I said to her on her second or third visit—when the hot flashes came back—that I thought the pains she'd been having were menopausal symptoms. She said, "I think I've known that intuitively for two years, but when I told the doctors, they didn't agree, so I stopped telling them."

Another woman came to me with irregular periods. This woman had always been very focused and clear-headed. But she had been experiencing this vagueness about herself—feeling as if she were surrounded by clouds. She said she was always confused. When she went to meetings she'd be unable to respond to questions. She found herself in the subway completely disoriented, not knowing where she was going. She had seen many doctors, and they labeled her condition depression and prescribed antidepressants, which did not help. I treated her symptoms, and two months later she came to see me and said, "I'm back to myself. I am me again." She was in menopause.

Homeopathy listens to the woman and looks at the symptoms.

Generally, the way I work with women who have menopausal symptoms is to follow them to see what's happening. I reevaluate every several months to see which symptoms have improved and which are persisting, and I adjust the homeopathic treatment accordingly. But if, after the first session, her condition has improved greatly, then often all that's needed is a follow-up several months later to adjust the remedies or a maintenance program that can take her beyond menopause.

With osteoporosis, however, determining a homeopathic remedy is difficult because there are no symptoms until the condition is well established. Patients with osteoporosis generally do not choose homeopathy as a form of treatment. Homeopathy would never make the condition worse, but we can't say if what we do arrests the condition or prevents it. It is an unknown. In general, with homeopathy, a menopausal patient can be helped to maintain a basic level of health that's acceptable and comfortable. That's what we know.

Homeopathy is not effective for encouraging lubrication of dry vaginal tissues, but if the dryness comes with itching or burning sensations, we can help relieve those symptoms. A woman always has the option of using a small amount of estrogen cream once in a while to relieve some of the dryness and revive the elasticity and lubrication inside the vagina. A menopausal patient of mine who is not comfortable using any form of estrogen has been using a nonestrogenic lubricant suppository called Replens—an over-the-counter product. She said she inserts it right before sex and that it works very well—she is not at all uncomfortable. I often learn from my patients. It's wonderful.

In my practice I don't recommend nutritional programs or exercise therapies because I do not have expertise in these fields. But I encourage patients to explore complementary therapies that can help them feel better emotionally and physically. By the way, vitamins and other nutritional supplements can be used while you are taking homeopathic remedies. Allopathic medications prescribed by physicians can be taken as well.

I have seen women thrive on estrogen replacement therapy. Sometimes the estrogen helps relieve some symptoms and not others, and then we add homeopathy to the estrogen therapy. Then there are women who have been told by their doctors that their medical problems contraindicate the use of estrogen, or they have tried it and experienced side effects and are looking for an alternative way to handle their symptoms. Homeopathy works, and because there are no side effects, it often works very well. But homeopathy functions on totally different levels from estrogen—it balances and stabilizes a body going through natural changes.

As a traditional homeopath, Dr. Elmaleh believes in personalizing the remedies she prescribes, with specific dosages for individual women, and is understandably reluctant to generalize her approach for menopause. However, I felt it was important for women to familiarize themselves with some of the names of remedies and how they are used. ("Marcia," page 181, who is under the care of a homeopath for menopausal symptoms, tells us what she is taking and the dosages prescribed by her doctor.) Also, in my research I found a few sources for homeopathic remedies often prescribed for menopausal symptoms. Dr. Trevor Smith recommends some homeopathic remedies for hot flashes in his book on homeopathy for women.[5] Here are some examples of Dr. Smith's recommendations. Notice how specific the symptoms are:

> ***Lachesis***
>
> Nearly always required at some time during homeopathic treatment of menopause. To be used when there is sweating with flushing and often violent headaches on top of the scalp. Symptoms may also include talkativeness and "intolerance of any form of constricting pressure to the body—like tight clothes."

Pulsatila

Needed for mild and variable symptoms of flushing, particularly around the face. The rest of the body "may be quite chilly. Tears are almost always present."

Kreosotum

Used when there is a problem with burning heat, combined with sweats that affect the whole body.

Author Diane Stein[6] mentions that "ignatia used two or three times a day" is a homeopathic remedy for hot flashes and constipation.

And mulimen[7] is another homeopathic remedy for menopausal women with typical symptoms: nervousness, depression, and hot flashes. According to a recent study, eighty-two women followed over a period of twelve weeks received doses of 40–60 and 80–100 drops of mulimen every day. "Very good therapeutic results were documented for 58.5 percent of the cases. Significant relief was especially apparent for the following symptoms: depression, nervousness, and hot flashes. The report recommended mulimen as the first medication of choice for treatment of menopausal symptoms."

Chinese Herbal Medicine and Acupuncture

Chinese herbal medicine, often accompanied by acupuncture, is an ancient system of healing whose principles have only recently been introduced to the United States with the opening up of China in the late 1970s. Chinese herbalist/acupuncturists like Teresa Xu began practicing in this country as private consultants. As more and more became known about the potential healing possibilities of acupuncture, Americans also began learning the techniques. Some traveled to China and enrolled in traditional schools; other took courses in this country or apprenticed with Chinese practitioners. Today most states have formal examinations—written and oral—to license those who want to practice acupuncture.

Herbal medicine as practiced by the Chinese is more difficult for Westerners to adapt. There are no schools for Westerners, and without written and verbal skills in Chinese, study is difficult. Also, many herbs are unavailable in the West and have to be ordered from China. A few Chinese herbs for menopause, like dong quai and ginseng, have been packaged by Western herb manufacturers and are available in most health food stores. But in general, anyone interested in Chinese herbs should see a practitioner.

Ms. Xu's office, like the offices of many acupuncturists, is set up with several long massage tables separated by curtains. Patients receiving acupuncture lie flat for twenty minutes to an hour, depending on the problem—anything from a common cold to anxiety, stress, and depression. The healing environment does not usually look like a medical doctor's office, unless the practitioner is American. I have been in treatment rooms in converted apartments or small spaces in office buildings; I have also received treatments in my home.

In general, it takes eight to ten treatments to affect a change. If nothing happens during that time, most acupuncturists feel another type of treatment may be required. Most recently, Ms. Xu has been giving me acupuncture "face lifts." The initial treatment program consists of one sixty-minute session once a week for eight weeks. When followed by an additional treatment every three or four weeks, the skin under my chin stays reasonably tight. It requires the use of many needles around the face, and I would not recommend it for people with very sensitive skin, but I've noticed the difference even when I'm unable to keep up the treatments.

Teresa Xu, educated in China as a traditional Chinese medical doctor, is now a licensed acupuncturist in this country. She apprenticed with a master physician for ten years, learning every phase of Chinese medicine. The training period was equivalent to the Western model involving medical school, internship, and residency. The progress of the student is monitored personally by a master, and he or she alone determines whether a student is ready for the next level of skill. To be accepted by a master is regarded as an honor, even though the hours are long and the work rigorous and demanding. Ms.

Xu's diploma certifies that she is trained in all the healing practices of Chinese medicine.

In China today, the government—advised by Chinese physicians—has formulated a standardized curriculum that is taught to anyone who wishes to learn traditional Chinese medicine.

During the Cultural Revolution in China, Ms. Xu was the medical doctor for a five-hundred-person factory, responsible for the total health care of the workers and their families. Days were often long and busy, and sometimes she would see as many as one hundred patients. With so many people to care for, personal attention was a luxury. Most complaints were taken care of quickly by dispensing herbs or, if necessary, using acupuncture. This demanding job gave Ms. Xu the practical depth of knowledge and the kind of experience that makes her a particularly flexible healer.

Ms. Xu's current practice consists of acupuncture, massage, and herbal medicine. Two years ago, Ms. Xu began the study of ch'i kong—the fourth and most esoteric part of Chinese medicine—with a renowned Chinese medical doctor, who is trained in Western medicine as well. It has added a dimension to both her personal and professional life.

Teresa Xu

It's difficult to explain our medicine to Americans because it is so different from yours. Based on Taoist philosophy, it holds that all the forces that operate in the universe also operate in human beings, and that there is an energy force in man and all living things that we call ch'i or qi. Ch'i circulates throughout the body and is what determines your health—the amount of ch'i, the quality of it, and how it is balanced influences everything. There must be a balance of ch'i not only in the body, but also between the internal energies and the world outside. Many things can influence or disrupt that balance: food, weather, climate, work, exercise. And with the instruments we have—acupuncture, massage, herbs, diet, and breathing techniques—we balance the individual body. But ch'i is not the only vital energy, although it is the most important. There is also one that influences blood, another body fluid, and another the life force. They all work together.

We believe yin and yang exist in all natural things. To maintain health in the body—as in the universe—yin and yang must be balanced. Yin is more powerful, but yin and yang depend on each other. Yin is female, negative, dark, passive, and carries the symbol of water. Yang is male, optimistic, active, positive, and its symbol is fire. In Chinese medicine, different organs of the body are characterized as yin and others yang. Herbs and food are also defined as yin or yang, and in treating patients we match the affected organ in the body with the appropriate medication or diet to achieve balance and health. But every body changes constantly, depending on so many things. The right diet for summer is not right for winter. Emotional stress or trauma can change a body's balance dramatically.

In our system there are ten vital organs that match Western anatomy and two "organs" that are Chinese and refer to energy. Each of them belongs to one of the five elements—earth, fire, metal, water, and wood—which are powerful natural forces that relate to each other as well as being either yin or yang. A yin organ is matched to a yang organ, and the organs are connected by meridians, or energy paths. The meridians—there are fifty-nine of them, although only twelve important ones—carry ch'i. When we use acupuncture on one of the main meridians or prescribe herbs, we want to reach the connected organ. Qi and the other energies connect the organs, the elements, and the meridians, carrying vitality to the whole body.

In Chinese medicine, we use a different method of diagnosis from that of Westerners. But, like Western doctors, the more people we examine, the more knowledgeable we become. Experience teaches us the subtleties of human illness and allows us to be more accurate in determining the problem. The diagnosis, however, is seldom a named disease as in the West—pneumonia, asthma, diabetes, and so on—which makes communicating with Western patients frustrating. According to our theory, menopausal problems are caused by a weakening of the various organs, causing an imbalance in yin and yang.

Yang excess or yin weakness or low energy or blocked circulation are typical of the diagnoses of problems we see. They may be the equivalent of pneumonia, asthma, or diabetes, but our treatment attempts to balance the body to overcome the imbalance rather than treat only the named symptom.

Talking to patients is part of the diagnostic process and very important. We need to know what they are feeling, what problems they're having. We listen to their voices. What is the quality of the voice? Weak? Strong? Tired? Are they breathing irregularly? Is there a cough? What kind of cough? And many other things. We watch behavior. How do patients hold their bodies? Are they nervous or jumpy? Do they seem anxious, moving all the time? We look at the color of skin, the texture. Is the skin dry or moist? In Chinese medicine, we do not take anything for granted. The way a body smells can be very important. Every part of the body and its changes can tell us something. We look at our patients' tongues—a normal tongue is pink and soft—to discover where the problems might be. Examining the tongue can give us many different clues to the state of the body.

We also use the pulse to diagnose. We feel six pulses on each wrist—they match the twelve important organs of the body. We read three at one time, pressing first lightly, then firmly. The pulses relate to the meridians. Some pulses are rapid, some are slow. Others are faint or strong. You learn to hear the differences clearly and know what the pulse means in combination with other clues.

There is no standard pulse reading that indicates normal health—everyone is different. For example, each menopausal woman is different, depending on her life-style, prior medical history, work, emotions, and so forth. And the treatment is designed specifically for that woman. Some women may only need acupuncture, others herbs. Some may need both and could also use massage. That is why it is so difficult to tell you specifically what we would do for an "average" menopausal woman. In Chinese medicine there is no "average"; every person is treated individually.

Acupuncture works to balance the body. We use thin silver needles and insert them in different places along the meridians. For example, in menopausal women, the kidney meridian often needs to be stimulated because the kidneys are related to the adrenals, which produce hormones like estrogen and progesterone. So when we talk about the kidney meridian, we mean not only the kidneys, but the organs that are influenced by that meridian.

Many times patients who have acupuncture for the first

time are fearful of the needles, but once they are familiar with the process, they relax. Often, acupuncture gives immediate relief from symptoms. Some people who have particularly sensitive skin complain when the tiny needle breaks the skin, but once it is in, they don't feel it. And right after treatment most patients feel very calm and relaxed. Sometimes women who have no obvious symptoms of menopause—hot flashes or night sweats—but are experiencing anxiety or depression or insomnia or nervousness can be helped by acupuncture. By the way, I use sterilized throw-away needles now because so many people are fearful of being infected by regular needles, even though sterilized.

Menopausal symptoms, like any other symptoms, are the result of a natural imbalance in a woman's body at this time. If her body is well balanced before menopause, the transition is usually not difficult. But if she has had hormonal problems in her younger years, we may have to work harder to stabilize her endocrine and nervous systems. To do this I often use herbs in combination with acupuncture, but again I design formulas for a woman's specific condition. Common Chinese herbs I've used are fu ling *(Poria cocos)* for women who are nervous or have problems sleeping; dong quai *(Angelica sinensis),* a very common herb used for hot flashes and one that also promotes circulation; he shou wu *(Polygonum multiflorum laulis),* good for relieving insomnia and also stimulating hormone production through kidney energy; ze xie *(Alisma),* also good for stimulating kidney energy and alleviating other female problems; wu wei zi *(Schizandra),* a hot flash herb that has an affinity for the kidneys and also balances fluids in the body.

I use massage when it is appropriate to treat patients. Traditional Chinese massage uses acupuncture points to increase or soften energy and balance the body. It works to achieve the same ends as acupuncture, but it is slower. Sometimes people feel more comfortable with massage than acupuncture.

When women's bodies are undergoing hormonal changes, massage is very useful, not only to relieve symptoms, but simply to relax the body and help improve circulation. Many women make massage a regular part of their health regimen, particularly when they are under pressure at work or are emotionally stressed.

In China many older women and men exercise daily—usually in the early morning—doing t'ai chi. The discipline requires very slow movement with strong control. You must concentrate on breathing as you move and work to keep yourself balanced. T'ai chi makes the body strong and gives you energy. Older people can maintain the flexibility of their youth if they exercise regularly, eat lightly, and take herbs to prevent disease.

Ch'i kong, an ancient Chinese breathing exercise designed to balance the energy in the body, is excellent for menopausal women. It's important to learn the exercise from a teacher so you are doing it correctly. A half hour or one hour a day can improve your body by balancing your major organs and will help you maintain your strength and increase your energy.

Diet is an important part of Chinese traditional medicine. Eating simply is best, with emphasis on fresh fruits and vegetables and grains. In general, I recommend eating very little meat or poultry—if at all—and then I would eat it combined with vegetables. The right foods balance the body and affect the mind and the spirit. Ideally, a woman whose hormones are changing should eat lightly and drink plenty of fresh vegetable and fruit juices and spring water to maintain a healthy balance.

By eating the right foods during the different seasons, we can help maintain the balance of yin and yang in our bodies. Spring and summer are yang seasons, while fall and winter are yin seasons. By making our bodies harmonious with the environmental changes of the seasons, we keep yin and yang in balance and support the strength of ch'i flowing through us.

Teresa Xu's Seasonal Dietary Recommendations

All Seasons

1. Morning physical exercise can strengthen our bones and muscles, improve circulation, keep us vigorous, and even prolong life. Before beginning your morning exercise, drink a cup of boiled spring water—warm. At night while we sleep, our bodies lose water through breathing and our skin. The bladder is full of urine, and our blood is thicker and moves more slowly. It is critical to drink water in the morning. Make sure it is warm; cold water is a shock to the system.
2. Women in menopause should have a bowl of lily soup several times a week to balance their hormones. In America it is often difficult to get fresh lilies, but any Oriental market carries dried lilies.

Recipe for Lily Soup

About 2 ounces of dried lily
Water
Honey

Soak the dried lilies in cold water overnight. Drain water and rinse until water is clear. Place lilies in a saucepan. Add water to cover and heat over a high flame until the water boils. Turn down flame and simmer for about 40 minutes, until the lilies are soft. Drain water, dry the lilies on paper towels, and eat with a spoonful of honey.

Spring

Eat lightly in the spring—using fresh foods and very little salt. Rice, wheat, and beans are good spring foods. Meat should be eaten sparingly.

Summer

When temperatures rise in the summer, our stomachs tend to digest food more slowly and our bodies perspire more. Watermelon, cucumber, eggplant, and black mushrooms will put back fluids into the body. Salt encourages our bodies to perspire even more, so eating less salt is advised.

Fall

The temperature is dropping, so we need foods that have more taste and give us more calories. Foods like eggs, fish, duck, bean curd, peanuts, celery, spinach, carrots, and corn can give us those calories.

Winter

Foods for the winter should give us enough calories to keep our bodies warm. The temperature of all the food we eat at every meal should be hot. Peanuts, soy beans, bean curd, seaweed, eggs, cabbage, and carrots are among the best foods for winter.

Exercise Therapy

According to all the practitioners interviewed in this book, the only therapy known at this time that can help women avoid bone loss and strengthen the heart is regular exercise. Mona M. Shangold, M.D., in an article in *Obstetrics and Gynecology*,[8] cites three studies on bone density and one on cardiovascular disease that supports the conviction held by Melanie Danza, an exercise specialist, and other practitioners that exercise is not optional for women who go through menopause naturally.

The first study conducted an eight-month exercise program—running, walking, and calisthenics—to discover its impact on the spines of sixteen healthy menopausal women. The control group comprised fifteen equally healthy nonexercising women. The results showed marked improvement in the bones of the women who exercised. Another study done on female swimmers and nonexercising women showed greater mineral content in the bones of the women who swam. The third study was done on fourteen menopausal women who followed a five-month program of arm exercises three times a week; the group who exercised increased the bone density in their arms, while the nonexercising control group lost bone density in their arms. The fourth study, cited by Dr. Shangold, on the impact of regular aerobic training—exercise done at a sustained elevated heart rate—concluded that both women and men could help reduce their risk of heart disease by exercise.

Women who are concerned about osteoporosis but prefer less strenuous exercise may be interested in a preliminary study (*Health Facts.* September, 1993) conducted at the University of Missouri at Columbia that showed no difference in the bones of the women who prefer to exercise moderately. The unexpected finding "was the lack of difference between low- and high-impact exercisers." This seems to point out that moderate exercise—walking, swimming, tennis, cycling, or any physical activity that adds up to thirty minutes or more at least five days a week—is "sufficient for women concerned about preserving bone strength."

Melanie Danza counsels menopausal and postmenopausal women who are clients of the Women's Wellness Center—directed by endocrinologist Dr. Lila Nachtigall, a proponent of ERT—on the appropriate exercise programs for their age and physical condition. Ms. Danza says that "the center addresses three specific women's issues: infertility, breast health, and menopause. But it also functions as a resource for most women's health needs. A woman can have her gynecological exam, get a mammogram, be tested for bone density, and consult a nutritionist, a psychologist, and an exercise therapist if she needs any of those services."

Women who do not take estrogen are often seen at the center for nutritional and exercise therapy, and they can take advantage of all the health services.

Formerly a ballet dancer, Ms. Danza ran her own dance school before studying aerobic exercise and weight-resistance training. She has been involved in the fitness world for nearly twenty years, associated with popular health clubs in New York City, and Reebok also recruited her to be a member of the Step Reebok National Training Team. Working with women, both nationally and internationally, convinced her that exercise is critical to maintaining good health and strength at every age, but particularly at menopause and in the years that follow, when hormone production diminishes and the body needs added support.

Ms. Danza's clients who are in menopause and need an exercise program come to her with an evaluation form prepared by a doctor that states the patient's cholesterol level, the results of her bone density test,* her age, and whether she is taking estrogen or not—all important to determining the type of exercise needed.

Melanie Danza

If a woman has low bone density and she is not doing any resistance exercise—putting bones under stress—I emphasize the importance of learning to work with weights to help increase the density. It is a fact that after forty-five bone density begins diminishing, and at menopause—even if you are replacing estrogen—bone loss accelerates. It is estrogen that helps produce vitamin D in the body, and it is vitamin D that helps absorb calcium, which strengthens the bones. If the body no longer produces D—because estrogen production declines—then calcium absorption is limited. There is a principle of exercise that is very important for women to understand: If you use your muscles in such a way that the

*This test measures bone density and requires the intravenous injection of a dye, followed by an X ray called a dual photon absorptiometry (DPA). The results are checked against the readings done on other women the same age.

bones are put under stress—namely, forced to resist or respond—then the size and density of the bones will increase.

A woman just beginning to work with weights could start with one-and-a-half pound weights, then work up to three pounds, and finally train with five-pound weights. Five pounds will put enough stress on the bones to increase density.

Numerous research studies have confirmed that exercise increases bone density; one study that was particularly revealing was conducted with eighteen women on Long Island. The women were two or three years beyond menopause. Bone density tests were done on all the women when they began the program. Then, half the women continued their normal sedentary life-styles. The other half exercised three days a week with weights and did aerobics. No changes in diet were made. No supplements were taken, nor was estrogen given. After eight months, bone density tests were done again on all the women. The results show that those women who exercised had increased the bone density in their spinal columns. On the other hand, density had deteriorated in the nonexercised group. I thought it was incredible. The facts are there—weight bearing and aerobic exercise, not estrogen, increased bone density.

Aerobic training is equally as important as resistance work because aerobics not only trains the heart to be a more efficient pump, but also creates impact on the skeletal system, which helps retard the loss of bone density.

When you do aerobic exercise, there are norms for different ages, and it's important that you work out within a certain range called your target heart rate zone. According to the American College of Sports Medicine, each person has an age-determined heart rate. Just subtract your age from the number

220. The result is your maximum heart rate—220 beats a minute is the speed of a baby's heart at birth. Multiply your maximum heart rate by 60 percent and 80 percent. This is your target heart rate zone, the intensity at which one needs to work to develop and maintain cardiovascular fitness. A fifty-year-old person like myself, who is aerobically trained and aerobically fit, may be able to work at a higher intensity.

Increasing bone density and being aerobically fit are not the only purposes of exercise for older women. It is equally important to make sure your muscles are strong. If you fall, strong muscles will protect weak bones from fracture. Women who increase their strength and remain flexible will be able to get through life easier. Bending down or reaching for things won't become chores for the body.

Women who do not take estrogen need to slow the process of bone loss with exercise even more than women who use the hormone (although all menopausal women need to exercise). Calcium and vitamin D need to be supplemented. We recommend 1500 mg of calcium—calcium citrate seems to be the best type to take because it's more easily absorbed by the body. Rather than 1500 units at one time, we recommend taking a supplement in the morning, maybe having a yogurt for lunch (for its calcium content), and completing the supplement or food requirement in the evening. Also recommended is 400 IU of vitamin D to help absorb the calcium.

Older women often choose swimming as an exclusive exercise because it's a comfortable activity. Personally, I think women need to do other kinds of exercise as well, even though some research exists now that indicates swimming, too, will help increase bone density.

The reality is, our bodies are meant to move. Exercise was not in the vocabulary of people a hundred years ago. If people lived outside of town, many walked the five or ten miles to work and back. And often the work they did was physically demanding. Exercise was an activity for the affluent—playing tennis or croquet. Today we seldom walk much, and often our work is sedentary, so we have to impose exercise on ourselves to get our bodies moving.

Cross training is a great way for older women to exercise. One day you might walk, the next day you might ride a bicycle, the third day go to a studio and take a low-impact aerobic class. These are all aerobic activities, but your body's working in different ways. If you do only one thing, like step training (stepping on and off a box at a regular pace) every day, eventually your body becomes so efficient that it actually uses less energy. Sometimes you have to trick the body to get it to work harder. If you love to run and that's all you do, then as you grow older the body will be overstressed by the high-impact forces to such a degree that you may have to stop running completely. Cross training running with a nonimpact activity like cycling, for example, will lower the risk of overuse injuries and add years to your running capabilities.

Although you can do both aerobics and weight training on your own, it's important to get some direction. Form and technique are essential to get the full benefits from working out. One of the best ways to ensure that you will do what is exactly right for you is to find a personal trainer. You don't have to hire one for the rest of your life. Work with the trainer for a few sessions or try a six-week course—once a week, until you know what you are doing. The local health club or exercise studio can probably help you find someone you can work with.

Reflexology and Pilates

These two approaches to body work are linked because they reflect a reality in alternative therapies—two or more specialized disciplines developed through personal interest and combined by a therapist into a single practice.

Roberta Kirchenbaum is one such specialist: a reflexologist who teaches the Pilates exercise method. Her colleague, Marika Molnar, is a physical therapist—a strong advocate of reflexology and the Pilates method who uses and recommends both to her clients as additional treatments along with physical therapy when it is appropriate.

The Ingham reflex method of compression, more commonly known as reflexology, is a healing method that applies pressure to specific areas of the feet called *zones* that relate to different organs of the body. It was introduced to the West in the 1930s by Eunice Ingham and is the method used by Roberta Kirchenbaum and most reflexologists today. Reflexology claims that by massaging a specific zone, the practitioner stimulates the sensory receptors below the skin's surface to send impulses through the body via the nervous system that can affect widely separated areas of the body. For example, one zone includes the kidneys and the eyes. It is believed that by stimulating the kidneys, the eyes, too, will be affected. Dark circles under the eyes have long been thought to be associated with a deficient kidney function.

Reflexologists generally work to balance the whole body, but the method can help alleviate specific health problems such as headaches, asthma, allergies, digestive disorders, and PMS.[9]

Based on yoga and calisthenic principles, the Pilates exercise system is named after its inventor, Joseph Pilates, who called it Contrology. Dancers were some of the first people to embrace his concepts. Pilates taught his students that exercise can develop both strength and flexibility. The exercises, done on specially designed equipment combined with mat work, are adapted to fit a woman's individual body needs. In the introduction to his book, *Return to Life*[10], Joseph Pilates says, "The art of Contrology proves that the only real guide to your true age lies not in years or how you think you feel, but as you actually are, infallibly indicated by the degree of natural and normal flexibility enjoyed by your spine throughout life. If your spine is inflexibly stiff at thirty, you are old; if it is completely flexible at sixty, you are young."

Roberta Kirchenbaum brought together her background, training, and interests to develop a practice that is unique to her talents. A former dancer, she teaches reflexology at the Manhattan Center for Living, a community health and human services organization that encourages alternative options for health care, and she also teaches the Pilates system of exercise to private clients. She talks about both in this interview.

Roberta Kirchenbaum

When I begin a reflexology session I place my client in a comfortable position with bare feet relaxed and raised to a level where I can easily work on her. Sometimes I sit or kneel, although most of the time I stand. The theory of reflexology is that if you put both feet or hands together and look at the bottom soles of the feet (or palms), they will map the organs of the body. Those organs on the right side of your body are on the right foot and those on the left are on the left foot. Based on Ingham's zone therapy, each toe line and each finger line is considered a zone. A zone begins at the top of the toe to the bottom of the foot or from the top of the finger to the wrist. We work by putting pressure on an area and then work up the toe or finger, and it is believed that the educated pressure will affect the organs, muscles, and nerves represented within that zone. Stimulated by pressure, the reflexes send the impulses through the nervous system and the spinal cord and effect physical changes.

Reflexology relieves stress and tension in the body by improving blood supply and allows nerve impulses to pass through blocked areas by releasing deposited toxins—a way of helping nature achieve homeostasis. On the simplest level, the physiological changes that happen in women's bodies during and after menopause are stressful to deal with. Relaxation of and for the body is healing, but it is difficult to relax when you are not feeling well. Stress is like a tourniquet on the nervous system that interferes with blood circulation, adding to a woman's physical discomfort. Reflexology opens up the passageways and allows the blood to flow freely.

Reflexology can also help to balance women's bodies as they change by giving support to the adrenal glands. The adrenals are particularly important at midlife because within the endocrine system the adrenals take over when the ovaries stop producing estrogen. Mind you, the adrenals are stress glands. In reflexology we stimulate the pituitary gland, the master gland in the endocrine system, which includes not only the adrenals but the thyroid, the parathyroid, the reproductive glands, and the pancreas. By stimulating the pituitary reflex in the big toe, we give support to the adrenals to do their work more efficiently. The adrenals have to work harder as the ovaries produce less and less estrogen over time.

A simple way for women to stimulate their own endocrine systems is to rub the Achilles' tendon, from the bottom of the heel, up the back of the calf, right up to where the Achilles turns into the gastrocnemius (it's where the calf broadens). Also, the area between the ankle bone and heel, on both the inside and the outside of the foot, can be rubbed every day. Some women find that it helps lessen mild hot flashes and relieves tension if done regularly.

As a reflexologist, it seems natural to begin balancing the whole body by starting with the feet, but I find that women, particularly older women, don't pay attention to their feet.

I always note what kind of shoe a woman wears and the condition of her feet. The fourth toe on the foot is known as the migraine headache toe, and I find that many, many women I work on who have really bad headaches are simply wearing the wrong shoes. Their toes in general are squashed, and the fourth toe especially is scrunched against that little toe. As I work on it, they report the headaches are relieved, and often the accompanying dizziness and fatigue fade away, too.

Many women need shoes with a little bit of a heel for balance, but I think it's important for women to be able to wiggle all their toes in their shoes. That's why the very best exercise for your feet is walking barefoot, particularly in the sand or on rocks. It's self-reflexology and very healthy for our entire bodies. The reflexology points for the head, brain, sinuses, and neck are all in our toes. It's hard for people who have never experienced reflexology even to imagine the ways it can help you feel better. You feel grounded, somehow. You walk differently because the whole foot is on the ground and you have a relationship to the earth.

Marika Molnar, my colleague, works primarily with dancers who regularly abuse their feet. She says she almost inevitably has dancers change their shoes when they come to her—not only the ballet slipper and the pointe shoe, but the street shoe as well. She says most people think that if they were a size 7 once, their shoe size will be 7 for the rest of their lives. But if you wore a size 7 at age sixteen, your feet may be a size 8½ by the time you're thirty-two because over the years your feet start to flatten to the ground—they widen and lengthen. Women are so used to stuffing their feet into shoes and holding them crunched, rather than articulating through the foot. So if women hold their feet, you can imagine all the reflexology points in the foot that aren't getting a daily massage through walking.

I also teach the Pilates method, privately, in my own studio. But the method is always personalized, even in larger studios where clients have individual programs and are watched carefully to make sure the exercises are performed correctly.

Pilates is a terrific exercise system for older women. It is a three-dimensional way to exercise that combines pushing, lifting, stretching, turning, and rotating through your spine, which can only make every other part of you very healthy.

The exercises, which are done on the mat or on the equipment, including a movable flat bed guided by springs, a stationary bed with bars, and suspended springs and other auxiliary pieces, are designed to work all parts of the body in different ways. The stretches and movements included in the method look like the stretches and movements of most exercise programs. But a combination of three factors makes Pilates a highly effective system: personal instruction, the special equipment, and the sequence of exercises individualized to strengthen the weakest parts while working on the whole body. As the body gets stronger and begins to achieve physical balance, varied and more difficult exercises are added to the regimen to further increase flexibility. Pilates is the only exercise system I know of that asserts it can condition your body to participate in the same activities you took for granted in your thirties and continue to do them for the rest of your life. Although no research exists to substantiate this claim, there is anecdotal evidence, particularly among older dancers, to prove the benefits of this system. Relatively unknown to a broad market ten years ago, the Pilates method is slowly becoming recognized outside the professional dance community. The system is taught in most major cities.

Marika Molnar is the director of Westside Dance Physical Therapy in New York City and director of Physical Therapy Services for the New York City Ballet. Her interest in the Pilates method developed out of her interest in therapies that help bodies move effectively.

Marika Molnar, P.T.

I have always been open to any exploration that was physically oriented, that would give me a deeper understanding of the body and new ways to work with it. I've studied many forms of body work—acupuncture, Rolfing, massage, and craniosacral therapy—and the knowledge I've gained contributes to my medically based practice of traditional physical therapy. I feel that using the knowledge of other disciplines and traditions is not at all incompatible with the hands-on body work I do in physical therapy.

When women's bodies are going through major changes, it is easy to attribute physical malfunctions exclusively to menopause, but some women are genetically a bit clumsy or uncoordinated, or they drop everything, or they're always getting injured. That may have more to do with not knowing where that joint is in space—a proprioceptive or kinesthetic sense. Your joints can develop that sense through controlled compression and decompression in a way that's not overly stressful. And that's where Pilates is effective: the system makes you aware of where all your joints are and what they are doing, and the amount of compression and decompression that is appropriate. It's not standing in place and doing jumping jacks. That's just not the way our bodies were designed to move.

Human beings are spiralers. Look at the way our pelvises work, see how our hips rotate. Physiologists, anatomists, and kinesiologists all know this, but perhaps it is such common knowledge to them that they haven't made the connection between this reality and the appropriate exercise to keep our bodies flexible and strong. This kind of movement is intuitive to the body but often forgotten, so teachers, guides, and advisers can only point it out to their students and then it is a student's responsibility to pay attention to his or her own body.

Women take for granted that decreasing bone density or osteoporosis is a natural consequence of growing older. This isn't necessarily so, but to prevent it from happening, menopausal women have to exercise. It's the only way to sustain their bones without taking estrogen. Weight-bearing activity will help maintain bone density, and I think one of the best exercises for this is walking. Recent articles on the astronauts noted bone mineral loss in their bodies because of floating in space without gravity. When we are upright, weight bearing, we are resisting gravity all the time, and that resistance sustains our bones.

I tell women to walk with a purpose, briskly, with a good movement pattern. Look at women or men after a certain age, and you'll notice that they tend to lose the ability to rotate their spines. When we walk, the movement of walking is naturally this cross-diagonal pattern—rotation. Older people often walk forward and backward, side to side. They need to learn to rotate again, and Pilates is very good for this.

Women need to know they are in control of their own bodies. We all have choices for exercise, and it depends on what we want. If you choose to have an iron-board stomach because when you go to the beach you want every part of your abdominals to be defined, then doing curls and crunches and sit-ups is great—it's what you should be doing. But doing crunches has no value or function in everyday life. And you should know that it's not a movement, nor does it have anything to do with your health. It won't really make your abdominals strong. The function of the abdominals is to stabilize the trunk. So even if you keep doing these crunches and have a washboard stomach, you can still injure your back because you didn't train the abdominals as functional stabilizers.

Pilates uses the abdominals to stabilize while the extremities are moving. Pilates also strengthens your body and enhances your own ability to go through a wide range of motions. It doesn't only strengthen you in a midrange. You get strength from the beginning to the end range, where the motion ends. And it's at the end range of motion—the place people are at their weakest—where they injure themselves. A pitcher actually gets injured just before the arm whips back because the most extreme range of motion is at the shoulder, and this is where players are weak. The Pilates method can strengthen the end range.

If you increase your lung capacity and heart capacity and the circulation throughout your system, your energy level increases. Exercise encourages circulation and nervous system involvement. And the way it involves the nervous system is by putting your brain and body together and making it work. Your nervous system gives you quick reflexes, allows you to make a quick change of direction, and keeps you moving at a certain speed instead of slowing down as you get older. In order to have a healthy nervous system, you need to exercise. You need to exercise to have healthy blood vessels, to keep pumping that blood back, refreshing and replenishing the body. It is absolutely essential during and after menopause.

For many women uncertain about what kind of exercise is most appropriate for them, I would recommend seeking out a specialist, someone who teaches a body-work system like Pilates, perhaps a chiropractor or a physical therapist. It makes sense that getting a professional analysis of your body before beginning an exercise program will make that program more effective. Experienced body workers can see the body imbalances from the way you walk. They can look at your spine and see where the curves are and whether you are restricted in any way, and they can help you make the adjustment.

Alexander Technique and Feldenkrais Method

The Alexander Technique and Feldenkrais method are physical disciplines that focus on the effects of the body on the mind and the mind on the body. Sarnell Ogus, a respected teacher of these two body/mind approaches, feels they can be of tremendous benefit to women during menopause and as they grow older, not to relieve symptoms but to explore how the perceptions we hold of ourselves affect us and can be changed by making changes in the way we hold our bodies.

The Alexander Technique was developed by F. Matthias Alexander around the turn of the century. Writers and intellectuals like George Bernard Shaw, John Dewey, and Aldous Huxley were impressed by this quirky new technique that seemed to alleviate chronic physical problems.

The Feldenkrais method was developed in the late 1940s by Moshe Feldenkrais, and among his prominent students were Margaret Mead, David Ben-Gurion, and Helen Hayes. Ms. Ogus, who trained with Feldenkrais, says he had studied the Alexander Technique as a young man, which probably accounts for the similarities between the two approaches. But Feldenkrais developed Awareness Through Movement and Functional Integration as original and evolutionary contributions to body/mind work. Both men taught how to release "habitual patterns" and develop alternatives. Both methods can be taught "one on one" or in a group.

Neither discipline is considered therapeutic, but the practice of either effects significant mental, emotional, and physical changes in the body.

At its simplest level, Alexander and Feldenkrais work to improve posture and breathing by identifying body habits. The awareness is what begins the process of modification. It sounds simple enough, but as Sarnell Ogus explained, "a habit is difficult for us to identify because a habit—which is performed repeatedly and mostly unconsciously—becomes familiar." It "feels right," even though it may be causing discomfort. By developing an awareness of how we hold our heads and bodies, we can affect the way the body moves and breathes and functions. That awareness will reveal to us the way we actually look at life, according to Ms. Ogus.

Sarnell Ogus not only teaches the Alexander Technique and Feldenkrais method, she also works as a Gestalt therapist. Her busy schedule includes training teachers—she is affiliated with NASTAT (North American Society of Teachers of the Alexander Technique)—and she is a senior faculty member of ACAT (American Center for the Alexander Technique).

"There are thousands of teachers of the Alexander Technique around the world," according to Ms. Ogus. "And Feldenkrais, too—although not as widely known—has an international following. Twenty years ago when I first began learning these processes, there were perhaps ten of us. Today, as more and more people are aware of the real changes that they can make in their bodies, we are truly coming into our own.

"In recent years," says Ms. Ogus, "there has been broad interest in both methods by physical therapists and orthopedists, who are often presented with problems that center around chronic neck pain, back trouble, and posture problems that are often difficult to relieve. And the results with both these disciplines have been impressive." When people take charge of their bodies, it's very empowering and hard to differentiate whether the change happens in the body or the mind. I think it's both.

My interest in the beginning was simply to improve my own posture; but the longer I talked with Ms. Ogus, the more I realized that knowledge of these approaches might be very important to other women in helping to deepen awareness of the connections among body, mind, and emotions as we age. If the way we carry our bodies has been imprinted on us by our minds—how we perceive, how we feel, how we see—then by improving our body awareness, we can remove the imprints. Could negative feelings and attitudes we have about aging add to the way we look, the way other people perceive us? Ms. Ogus believes it does. If, for example, "you hold an unconscious belief learned from mother or grandmother that everything is over at menopause, you're going to walk around like everything is over. Your body will reflect that attitude," she says.

The Alexander Technique changes the way you perceive yourself and ultimately gives you self-confidence. The physical body holds the ideas, perceptions, and emotions of the mind and the psyche in its muscles, tendons, and bones. By changing the body, you can change the way you think. Experiencing this method personally can literally change not only your body, but your life.

Sarnell Ogus

I was trained as a dance therapist. But when I was in my late thirties I was in a cab accident on the way to a dance class that resulted in headaches, general body aches, and eventually a herniated disk. I spent two years searching out the most conventional forms of medical treatment around. I was in excruciating pain, and the only relief I found was by following an exercise program recommended by a prominent back specialist. But I continued to live on Valium.

My condition deteriorated until I was almost crippled and needed the support of a cane to walk.

Then a woman I met by chance at a party told me about the Alexander Technique. I had never heard of it, and I thought, That's so flaky. But something she said to me began to click, and I actually began to think about my spine, what a herniated disk was, and how an accident that seemed minor had precipitated the problem.

Two weeks before I was scheduled for surgery for a spinal fusion, I consulted a teacher of the Alexander Technique. The teacher explained what she observed about my body. The observation was a revelation. Simply by correcting the way I held my body, I could finally participate in my own well-being. I didn't have to be a victim of what was going on around me. No one had done this to me; my body was doing this. There was a change in the pain almost immediately. But it took perhaps eight months for the pain to diminish significantly. And then after a few more months of almost no change, I made a tremendous leap and was really completely free from pain. I never did have the surgery.

I now draw from the Alexander Technique, Feldenkrais method, and Gestalt therapy in my therapeutic practice, depending on the needs of my students. When I first began doing this kind of work, our rule of thumb was a lesson for every year of your life. But that isn't strictly true because people have different abilities to learn and different ways of learning. Some older people learn better and faster than younger people. So we set ten lessons as an arbitrary number.

I observe a student very carefully when she comes to me. I ask her to perform simple tasks: to pick up something, sit down on a chair and get up, walk across the room, and so on. Then with touch and words I teach students new and better habits for their bodies. I often work with musicians. They'll bring their violins or clarinets, and I'll put my hands on them and guide them so they can feel the difference between their old stance and the new position, allowing them to have balanced bodies.

As people grow older they tend to hold their heads and necks in a controlled way. It may have to do with fear—fear about being old, fear about falling—so they freeze the neck. The neck is the main stem of the spine, and all the nerves are up at the very base of the skull and go into your brain, into the scalp, and you lose a certain amount of circulation. When we free the neck, there is more ease in the body. The circulation improves. Breathing improves. Students have more energy.

We have a model in the Alexander Technique called Primary Control, which refers to the way the head is balanced on the neck and torso. And the challenge is for the head to remain balanced no matter what tasks we are performing, whether it's washing the dishes, riding a bike, or even sitting and watching television.

We have to be aware of how we are functioning, and that is very difficult because the body turns everything into a habit. Kinesthetically, the habit informs us visually of what's around us. When you try to change the way you hold your body, you are changing your whole relationship to life.

If you have held your head tilted to the right with your shoulder up for a lifetime, it distorts the way you see and the way others see you. If we change that, it can be very disturbing, because it will look wrong and you'll find you can't trust your kinesthetic perception. This analogy, of course, applies to many ways we look at life.

When you use the Alexander Technique, you open up the whole area of respiration. Your diaphragm becomes freer, you also breathe more easily, your lungs work better, your heart works better, your circulation improves. Your joints stay open. Sometimes you'll see women or men with a dowager hump that could be attributed to osteoporosis, but it may simply be an unconscious compaction of the spine. These are people who have never thought consciously of their relationship to gravity, so they let their bodies fall. Of course, as you age there is a certain amount of sagging, but it can be minimized by conscious awareness of the relationship of the head to the neck to the torso. If you learn that basic principle, the body will fall into place.

Now, of course, I teach more than that, and most Alexander teachers do, too. People need to know more. They have to understand the mechanics of using the whole body. Many old people walk mechanically and stiffly; they don't understand that they can move from their hip joints. They are unaware of their own physical possibilities. Many people both young and old are locked in the pelvic area. When the head is balanced on the body, it allows the body to move more easily, particularly the spinal column and all the major joints—the hips, the shoulders.

When I put my hands on people, I can feel the way their bones are organized and what's going on in their bodies, which may be a manifestation of how they are thinking. When you worked in the traditional Alexander way, it wasn't important to understand why your body adapted those habits and ways of functioning. But, personally, I feel if you understand why, you can make more organic changes.

Feldenkrais, too, did not feel that the model of Primary Control—at the core of the Alexander Technique—was enough. He worked with the total body in a process more like physical therapy. He moved the body with the intention of bringing awareness and consciousness to the mind, to identify the habit. Once the habit was identified, he went about introducing a better habit. The better habit is developed by physically moving the limbs in the optimum way so that the nervous system gets stimulated and the brain begins to form new information about how to function.

The remarkable thing is that with awareness, the changes can happen in the body. But of course the difficult part is achieving the awareness. When people begin the work, sometimes they find they can't sit on a chair in a simple way. They have developed a habit of sitting in a way sometimes so detrimental to their bodies and themselves that when they become aware of the habit, they are shocked it could have happened.

Eventually the awareness is like a mantra that allows you to keep a sense of yourself. "Neck free. Let your neck be free. Let your head move forward and up. Let your torso lengthen and widen."

If someone comes to me for the Feldenkrais method or the Alexander Technique, I will begin working with them, but as often happens, emotional material emerges because everything is locked in the body. I will say to them, "I'm a therapist, and if you like, we can process this material, or you may wish to go to someone else." Other psychotherapists often refer to me patients who are blocked or stuck. Helping them work through something physically in their bodies often releases the block and can push them along in the psychotherapeutic process.

Personally, I believe that people have different ways of learning. The Alexander Technique was a mission for me because I had personally experienced its benefits. But as I began working with people, I realized that some learned better with Feldenkrais, which is more nonverbal. Alexander is very verbal. We talk a lot to our students. We assist them in thinking. With Feldenkrais, we move people and don't say much. But both methods work to the same end: to allow a person to make choices about how she or he wants to be. No one needs to be stuck in any pattern. Having made changes in the physical body, you know you can affect the choices you make in work or relationships, for example. Even if you have limitations or handicaps, you have more choices than your handicap informs you that you have. You could say that menopause or aging is a handicap and that's it. You'll live with it or accommodate it. But there are lots of choices. The way you think, the way you eat, the way you exercise, the way you make up your mind about anything in your life—you have choices.

Body awareness, a natural reaction for young women, is even more essential for women in their forties and fifties and, like myself, in their sixties. Because, inevitably, our bodies will change beginning with menopause. If we understand that we can do something about the speed and the course of that aging, it will not happen to us in the same way.

It's not so much that I want to look young or stay young. I'm not so interested in that at all, because if you stay young, you stop living. I want to be young in the moment-to-moment, in the way I look at things. It's not appropriate for me at my age to look at life with forty-six-year-old eyes. At sixty-seven, if I let myself be who I am, then everything I experience is a new experience. No, I don't want to stay young, I want to be young.

Affirmative Self-Hypnosis

Body/mind techniques, useful at any time, are particularly interesting explorations at midlife, when so many real physical changes are happening in the body, along with the related emotional and psychological responses. Learning to use self-hypnosis is a valuable exercise that extends to controlling menopausal symptoms and beyond, to increasing self-confidence in work and personal relationships. Dr. Marcia Greenleaf uses a method of self-hypnosis on herself and taught it to me in a single session. Self-hypnosis is not necessarily a therapeutic treatment, but it can be used in a therapeutic way. I do believe that when used in combination with other treatments for relieving menopausal symptoms, it can lessen the intensity of those symptoms and can be most effective in relieving anxiety and stress.

This original form of visualizing an ideal situation is a drug-free way to deal directly with the many issues women face as they age—issues ranging from hot flashes or the stress of divorce to making a career change. Dr. Greenleaf says that some people need more skill training than others, but often the technique of self-hypnosis can be achieved in one or two sessions.

Dr. Greenleaf is a noted psychologist specializing in behavioral medicine and clinical hypnosis. She currently works on staff with cancer patients at the Evelyn H. Lauder Breast Center at Memorial Sloan-Kettering Hospital. Dr. Greenleaf also maintains a private psychotherapy practice in which she teaches her patients how to use self-hypnosis as a therapeutic tool for refocusing the mind and changing attitudes.

Marcia Greenleaf, Ph.D.

In one session, someone can be assessed for how easily they can be hypnotized, taught how to enter and exit from a trance, and taught a therapeutic strategy—what to focus on. In my work, I like to have a follow-up session because people have questions and may need reinforcement or fine-tuning on the method. If someone is stuck emotionally or her motivation is not as strong as she thought, she may need more sessions—not to learn hypnosis but for psychotherapy. And the time spent in these sessions is about working through whatever may be blocking her from working with the self-hypnosis.

There are very different aspects to the trance state. It can be very quiet, very internal, and can produce a kind of receptivity and deep relaxation where you don't feel like moving—a kind of reverie or refuge. Or it can be like an alert, awake state of concentration in which you have a double consciousness. For example, if I am to give a lecture, but I have been racing around with my mind on a million other things, I put myself in a trance before beginning my lecture. I am alert, awake, and focused exclusively on my ideas. This technique improves my performance and allows me to interact with the audience. Without the trance state I'd worry about what people are going to think, whether I can remember everything. I'm not really there. I may not listen as alertly to what people ask me or remember very specifically what I've said.

Think about going into trance as a way to quiet the static in the nervous system so that our connections on all levels—metaphysical, emotional, and psychological—are more efficient. This technique frees us up to be who we are. Every woman can think of a time when she had a headache or a hot flash that upset her so much that she couldn't think straight. The trance state makes it possible to think more clearly.

Hypnosis is a way of learning to focus your attention, to allow you to pay attention to a single theme, idea, image, or feeling in such a way that whatever else is going on around you fades away. It allows you to use your mind like a psychological zoom lens, so that what you zoom in on begins to fill the field of your consciousness. What you choose to fill that field with can affect certain physiologic processes in your body or emotional states or decision making. And when that happens, behavior changes.

I compare the process to watching television. You are simply sitting there quietly, and you've got a box in front of you with light and sound and images. As you look at it and hear it, what you hear and see has an effect on your total being. If you see something upsetting, you can be overcome with sadness. Watching something terrifying can cause your heart rate to change, affect your digestion, and leave you very tired. On the other hand, watching something inspirational excites and energizes you. Self-hypnosis teaches you how to use your mind as your own internal TV, where you choose the frequency, the picture, the sound, and the mood that works for what you want to achieve—what your goals are.

I ask my patients to imagine a large split screen. The left side of the screen is used for projecting worries, self-criticism, fears, hot flashes, night sweats, and anxieties. You take them out of the body so they won't create static and intensify difficulties. The greater right side of the screen is the creative side. Your sense of balance and harmony, your goals, are up there. This way you can organize, direct, balance, or explore what's going on without turning your body into a battlefield.

Most people do a kind of self-hypnosis on themselves all the time. But we do it negatively. We bring in fear thoughts: Oh, my God, I don't want *that* to happen. I know I'm going into that meeting and I'm going to have a hot flash. Or, I won't sleep again tonight. Recognition of those thoughts is all that's needed. I say, "Let me change that thought. Let me focus on what I want, how I want it, and what feelings I want to encourage myself to bring up." This we can do by ourselves. Where we need help—why people come to me—is in becoming aware of the negative suggestions we give ourselves or shedding light on the insecure feelings we have about our possibilities.

When someone is in a negative state for any reason, she needs help in three ways. One is to recognize when she is going into spontaneous trance states—being absorbed in one's own thoughts and feelings (like a daydream). Two is to learn to identify the negative thoughts. Three is to learn how to go into trance on purpose—like a state of meditation—and then focus on helpful strategies and possibilities. The purpose is to use the trance state to enhance the mind/

body communication by paying attention to what you are "for" rather than what you are "against" or afraid of.

Sometimes how the mind/body connection works seems very abstract, so let me give you a more concrete example. When a dancer is learning how to do a pirouette, in order not to fall over, she has to carry an image in her mind that represents a sense of balance. If she thinks she is going to fall over, she will fall over. If she thinks she can't turn around more than once, her body gets the wrong instruction. The image of balance will direct her body to do the pirouette. If a professional golfer thinks a shot is going to go to the left, the body gets the message "to the left," and that's where the ball goes. If a woman gets a trigger for a hot flash and, instead of fighting it, she thinks "cool," her body can respond to the thought of coolness.

Hypnosis can alter physiology—control blood pressure and bleeding, affect heart rate, clear complexions, and more. We know this. But we never know when we start with a person to what degree they are going to be successful. Some people are able to do it a hundred percent, but what we don't know is how much of it is related to motivation, hypnotizability, or the exact nature of how much the physiologic balance is altered. But for women who can't take hormones and don't want to use drugs, hypnosis will certainly help balance the body.

It seems to me, however—and I can't make this point strongly enough—that all women owe it to themselves, whether they use hypnosis as a vehicle or not, to use this change of life as a time to focus on everything that has to do with health and well-being. Women tend to ignore the fact that hot flashes are dehydrating. It's the time to drink eight glasses of water a day, not counting coffee or diet soda. Paying attention to diet is more important than ever before. If you don't eat all day and drill your body into a starvation mode, and you expect hypnosis to correct the effects on your body, you're asking too much of yourself.

Now, that's up front. Any woman who comes to me for hypnosis to treat hot flashes or vaginal dryness gets the standard "how to take care of your body" explanation before we get to hypnosis. Then, here's what I teach them. Using the hypnotic state, you can focus on certain kinds of images that control body temperature and circulation. If the problem is hot flashes, the self-hypnosis suggestion to the person is to allow her body temperature to become comfortable, stable, and soothing. But for the suggestion to be effective when a hot flash occurs, she needs to practice working with her body in this new way on an ongoing basis and not just wait until she has the hot flash.

Most women get a trigger before a hot flash—slight dizziness or slightly upset stomach. That's the time to go into a hypnotic state and imagine the body being cool—cool and comfortable. Some women imagine themselves in the snow. If they're skiers, they can put themselves on the ski slope. Other people can imagine they are walking into a refrigerator. The image and suggestion is very personal because everyone has different settings and environments in memory that mean something to them. Depending on the degree of hypnotizability, a person will need to make more or less of an effort to actually produce the feeling. Women who are at the low end of hypnotizability can work with the image and suggestion and not get the feeling right away, but if they continue to practice, they will still make the body connection. The process can be helped by touching a real ice cube or cold water. It isn't cheating to help our imaginations work!

If you learn to hypnotize yourself to keep your mind and body balanced and you combine that skill with eating properly, drinking water, and treating vaginal dryness with vitamin E, the mind and body work together to maximize nutritional intake and increased fluid intake. We can control the functions of the body with our minds. The principle is fundamental to healing.

The long-term benefits of self-hypnosis are different for everyone. The balance that you will get for any given day may not last—we create it, we lose it, but we can re-create it again. The wonderful thing about having self-hypnosis available to you is that you constantly re-create and make adjustments for better balance and a sense of mastery over negative feelings and fear.

Aromatherapy

Aromatherapy can be traced back to ancient Egypt, Greece, and Rome, where there is evidence that exotic essential oils were used therapeutically as medicine. The Bible often mentions using oils to restore people emotionally.

The use of essential oils was revived in the 1920s by French chemist Rene Gattefosse who coined the word *aromatherapy* and wrote the first modern book on the subject. But despite its early origins and its more recent revival, aromatherapy is still considered new among the more traditional alternative therapies such as acupuncture or chiropractic. However, if we do accept the healing value of herbs, the logic of aromatherapy makes sense. Oils from the leaves, flowers, and roots of plants with curative properties, when inhaled or massaged into the skin, work the same way herbs and vitamins taken orally can heal the body.

Aromatherapists like Christine Henrich believe that the essential oils act even faster when ingested than inhaled or applied to the skin because they are absorbed directly into the bloodstream.

Ms. Henrich introduced me to a massage with essential oils. The oils made the massage decidedly more relaxing, and it was my experience that the effects lasted longer than a massage without oils. My reasons for having the massage were not menopausal, but the usual reason for a writer: tight neck, shoulders, and back, and aching legs from wrapping them around each other unconsciously when I work, discomforts that increase with age. If a massage sybaritic enough to be offered as a service to clients at spas and health resorts is also therapeutic, the benefits should diminish any impulse to dismiss it as a luxury. Massage is not a luxury for women whose lives are stressed and whose muscles need relaxing from the tightness that can exacerbate menopausal symptoms. Therapeutic massage differs from a beauty massage in that muscles, tendons, internal organs, and the lymphatic system are stimulated at the same time the body learns to relax.

A graduate of the Pacific Institute of Aromatherapy and a licensed massage therapist, Christine Henrich combines both these disciplines in the practice of aromatherapy massage. Europeans emphasize the therapeutic value of oils, although in this country they are used primarily for personal enhancement. "In Europe the oils are used as medicine, as originally intended," Ms. Henrich remarked, "and the practice of aromatherapy is even covered by insurance in France. Scientific research continues to confirm that many essential oils have been proven to have healing properties, and there is work going on to broaden their medicinal application. Medical doctors in France and, I believe, also in Switzerland administer the oils orally and through injection, just the way they now use intravenous antibiotics."

Currently, in the United States there are no studies to prove the effectiveness of the use of essential oils in a therapeutic setting, although the anecdotal response by people who have used oils is very positive. Aromatherapy is one of the fastest growing natural healing arts.

Christine Henrich, M.T.

Aromatic oils work not only to improve the body's health, they work psychologically, too. They are mood elevators that can really lift your spirits and relax your mind. When a scent is inhaled, it activates the part of the brain that regulates emotions. Smelling something you find pleasant can trigger pleasant memories. It can turn your mood around within a few seconds. The trick is to find the right scent, because what I find pleasant may not be so for someone else.

Essential oils are extracted from different parts of the plant—the roots, leaves, petals of flowers, skins of fruit, and so forth. They exist in small sacs between the cells of plants. They contain vitamins, hormones, antibiotics, and antiseptics and are much more concentrated than herbs. The distilling equipment to extract the oils is often installed in the flower field because the flowers used have to be picked during a specific season and at a certain time of day to get the highest quality of oil.

Oils range in price from three dollars to several hundred dollars for a half-ounce bottle. For example, it takes about three hundred pounds of rose petals to make one ounce of rose oil. So of course it's going to be costly; a half ounce of rose oil costs about $300, but you can buy one-sixth ounce for about $80. The good thing is that you don't have to use expensive oils like rose and jasmine regularly, although they are really wonderful. You can find less expensive oils that fit your budget and also work well.

The practice of aromatherapy is very technical when used therapeutically, which is probably one of the reasons there aren't many of us doing it. Mixing the oils, like formulating a good perfume, is an art. Some oils can be toxic (usually they have to be ingested in large doses for this to happen), but care must always be taken, and only pure and natural oils should be used. If you want the blend to be effective, you have to know what you're doing. You want to create a balance. You don't want to use two oils that cancel each other out. If, for example, one is very energetic and the other very sedating, don't take them together because you won't get the effect you're after. You also want to know what scents work together—how intense one odor is compared with another. The odor of chamomile oil, for example, is seven times the intensity of that of lavender oil, so you're not going to mix it in equal parts because the chamomile will be overpowering: all you will smell is chamomile. But anyone can easily and safely make a blend for the bath or as an inhalation.

Researchers are finding that our brain waves change when exposed to certain scents, and our behavior is affected accordingly. For example, smell used effectively can ease stress. When oils and massage work together, the benefits can be achieved faster than by using herbal remedies because the oils are absorbed through the skin during a massage.

We begin an aromatherapy massage session by discussing the client's symptoms. If they are menopausal—hot flashes, depression, mood swings, anxiety, and so on—I combine oils suited to relieving those symptoms. But it's important that the oils smell good to the woman. What one woman finds pleasant another may not, so I prefer to blend my oils at the time of the massage.

Soon after the massage begins, a person starts to feel better and more relaxed because the oils are absorbed through the skin. And the scent is on the body for two to three hours after the massage is over. It's really not a quick fix because you can feel the effects of the oils even a few days later. They work to help your body regulate itself. The effects of an aromatherapy massage generally don't last for more than a week, but to extend them I often prepare oils for clients to take home and use in a bath.

If a woman has severe menopausal symptoms, weekly aromatherapy massage treatments are necessary for lasting results. But if you are looking for a quick fix for mood swings, an occasional massage can help. Once you become aware of your body, you'll begin to know how long the effects last and can adjust your schedule.

I believe in herbology. I know it works therapeutically, but I prefer working with essential oils for massage therapy. Massage therapists have to know the body. Anyone can use massage to help someone relax, but real knowledge of anatomy and physiology is essential if you are going to use it therapeutically. Also, as a massage therapist I try to help people get in touch with their own bodies. I try to make them aware of where they hold stress and how much better they can feel by alleviating the stress. We can't do away with it completely, but regular massage can help keep the muscles relaxed and prevent tension from building up.

The therapeutic value of massage, even without the oils, is beginning to be recognized. A good massage increases the circulation of blood and lymph fluids and assists in the removal of toxins. All organs of the body—skin, muscles, nerves, and organs—are stimulated by massage. I use a basic Swedish style, although I add acupressure and reflexology when applicable, always taking into account the client's needs. I prefer to use more fluid movements and soothing techniques when working with menopausal symptoms. You want to get the oils into the body and relax the client.

The benefits of essential oils for normal menopausal symptoms do not have to be combined with massage to be effective. For hot flashes a woman can just put a few drops of clary sage in a mister bottle with spring water and spray herself; she'll cool off quickly. Clary sage has also been very effective for lifting your spirits when you're feeling depressed. And pricewise it's in a middle range. I often use it in aromatherapy massage on women in menopause because research suggests that clary sage contains elements that may be transformed by the body into estrogenic factors. Traditionally, fennel and sage have been used by women in menopause to help regulate estrogen production by massaging the oils on their abdomens or lower backs.

Rose oil and jasmine, too, can be used both to lift you out of a depressed state and to regulate the female reproductive organs. Again, you can massage the oils on the abdomen or lower back, or you can mix a few drops with water and use either oil in a douche. Essential oil of bergamot, geranium, rosewood, and clary sage can also help ease mood swings when used in a bath.

If you use these oils in spray form or inhalation, they won't change your life, but they can get you past that really bad wall when you just don't know what to do with yourself, and once you've achieved a balance, you can move on from there.

Diet and Nutrition

Most of us do know what we should and shouldn't eat, but during menopause women are often more stressed physically and consciously eating well becomes more important. Some women gain more weight than they'd like, even though their diets remain the same; others lose weight. And it's all due to shifting hormones.

Generally, diet experts agree that eating less and eating lightly is wise anytime, to ease the body's work, since digestion is one of the hardest jobs your body performs. But at menopause we also can lighten the body's responsibilities by making better food choices.

A word of caution when selecting a nutritionist. A good nutritionist understands the biochemistry of the body and works to balance it through the use of foods and food supplements. The growing interest in eating healthfully has given the generic title of "nutritionist" high visibility and cachet, and people who seek out such professionals should be aware that some dietitians are adding the generic appellation "nutritionist" to their earned title—R.D., registered dietitian. They may know how to balance meals for institutions, but may not be as knowledgeable about balancing your body.

Dr. Jeffrey Sullender, a specialist in nutritional biochemistry, relates to healing from that perspective, and in the course of the interview that follows, he offers his recommendations. The field of nutritional biochemistry—balancing the body chemistry by using foods and nutrient supplements—was unknown to Dr. Sullender when he left his premed biology studies at age twenty-two because of chronic relapsing pancreatitis. "My health was failing so miserably, so rapidly, that I had to find some sort of alternative to reverse my decline," says Dr. Sullender. "Once every six months I'd be in the hospital, and for years I was on codeine for pain and Compazine for nausea, Valium for nerves and Dalmane for sleep." He consulted a variety of doctors, until the last physician, a gastroenterologist dealing with disorders of the digestive system, explained that they simply could not find the cause for his symptoms and were unable to help him. Having exhausted all his medical resources and getting worse, he began the exploration and formal study of nutritional biochemistry and alternative medicine that eventually brought him back to health.

"I was lucky that my strong biology background helped me understand the implications," Dr. Sullender declares. "I started reading books and talking to researchers, clinicians—many, many people. The 1970s was an early time for seeking out alternative therapies, but little by little I put the information together, and over the next few years I found most of the answers for my health. And I've been well since—maybe not 100 percent, but I can function, work, contribute to and enjoy life. I was forced to learn it all the hard way, which I did! The experience was a good teacher, but a very tough one."

A certified clinical nutritionist and a member of the board of directors of the International and American Associations of Clinical Nutritionists (IAACN), Dr. Sullender also serves on the IAACN Scientific Advisory Council and lectures widely in both academic and business circles on nutritional biochemistry. Today he devotes his time to teaching, writing, and his practice in nutritional biochemistry and natural health care.

Dr. Sullender uses an integrated approach to treat all body imbalances, among them menopausal symptoms. Once the source of the problem is located, he uses nutrition as a focus and then supplements his recommendations for diet with herbal and vitamin therapy and homeopathy, when appropriate, to bring a body back to health.

Jeffrey S. Sullender, Ph.D., C.C.N.

Nutrition is not an alternative therapy. It is core and fundamental to everything else you do for your body. The original word for diet was *diaita,* which is Greek for "life-style." To the ancient Greeks it meant not only what you ingested foodwise, but what you took in emotionally and intellectually. It was an all-encompassing word to represent the way you lived your life. And now it's been distorted into meaning a four-week period of deprivation and then a return to normal eating. The concept has created all kinds of problems. People haven't learned how to eat healthfully. They have not learned the laws of nature we all must follow or pay the consequences.

If it is sometimes difficult to eat the right foods, it is encouraging to know that when you do, your cells can change—even though the process is slow. So there is always hope that you can make the next cell function better than the current cell. By making better food choices, there is real opportunity for improvement. The body has a tremendously resilient, self-regulating capacity, if we will only give it a chance.

It's important to understand that a good nutritionist doesn't treat disease. We work to improve health and to remove the blocks that may impede health. If body functioning is balanced, obstacles removed, and the biochemistry of the body near optimal, the body should treat the disease.

The traditional definition of health is the "absence of disease"—a negative definition that says if the body shows no signs of disease presently detectable, then by default the body is healthy. Unfortunately, that's a very uninspiring concept! How many Americans go to their physicians with complaints of gas and bloating, some minor bowel problems, skin eruptions, and headaches now and then? They have blood tests and are pronounced "healthy." "No disease present," say the reports. But no one discusses the fact that there is a whole range of preclinical, predisease states that are not healthy. People often come in to see me and announce, "I'm overweight, I've got bad skin, I've got PMS, but otherwise I'm 'perfectly healthy.' " If you have such an array of symptoms, but are healthy, then what is health? We need to define it as a positive state of well-being, characterized by a buoyant energy, clarity of mind, and the ability to adapt in life. In Chinese medicine there is an old proverb: "Health is the silence of all the organs."

It is important to have a thorough and extensive health history when evaluating a woman for menopausal symptoms. I like to know her past medical issues, her symptoms, her complaints over the years. Any infections, surgery? What is her life-style? Dietary habits? Does she eat foods with high nutritional content? What kind of work does she do? Is she sedentary or active? Is there a family history of osteoporosis? There are many, many factors to consider. One variable, such as replacing estrogen, will not give you the key to balancing a woman's body at menopause. There are many keys and many locks. We have to look at the whole pattern. We not only have to talk about the current symptoms and how long those symptoms have been apparent, but whether they have caused other symptoms to surface.

For example, a woman may be in menopause, but she also may have had fifteen years of digestive problems. Maybe the problem is constipation. That will be a factor in how the body handles the change in hormones. We can't separate out the digestive function from the menopausal complaint, because absorbing the right nutrients—zinc, magnesium, or fatty acids—to make, use, and eliminate the hormones correctly is fundamental to addressing the complaint. We can't treat the symptom and ignore the digestion. We have to look at why the digestion is out of balance and if that is having a nutritional impact on hormone status.

That doesn't mean we ignore the symptoms; of course we work to eliminate them by virtue of correcting the causes. The important goal of biochemical nutrition is to rebalance the whole body. Some people set very limited goals and look only for temporary relief, and they're happy with that. But most women understand, once it is explained and discussed, that getting to the root cause of the symptom is important to how their bodies function beyond menopause.

For example, if a thyroid is not producing enough hormone, we ask why, as any other practitioner might do. But in this field we try to find out if certain nutritional problems or stresses within the individual might be causing that altered thyroid function. Making up the deficit by supplying an outside prescription of synthetic thyroxin may work faster, but by doing that, we haven't uncovered the real problem. The ovaries, too—even when intact—may not be putting out enough estrogen or may be producing too much estrogen. Before recommending hormones, we would prefer to get the best sense of where the problem originates and try to address it, naturally.

That's why case taking is a real skill, almost an art form. It's both intuitive and deductive. A well-taken case history should provide a sense of where the problem originated. Again, back to our simple case of constipation. If you're someone with chronic headaches and intolerance for digesting fats and oils and prone to chronic constipation, the symptoms might well link back to that. Sometimes by correcting the digestion alone a woman's body will spring back with real resilience and the hormones will balance themselves. Remember, everything is interconnected in the body—it's one system of systems!

The current medical approach to menopause is to recommend hormone replacement therapy to nearly all menopausal women, with or without symptoms, who are free of risk factors. From a biochemical perspective I feel strongly that women need to understand how the endocrine regulatory loop functions in order for them to make decisions regarding treatment for symptoms or to rebalance their bodies during this natural biochemical change.

There are three critical parts to the endocrine loop. First are the hormone-producing organs or cells—ovaries, adrenals, thyroid, and so on. Hormones like estrogen and progesterone and many others are carried by the bloodstream to the second part of the loop—the cells that are programmed to receive the hormones and use them. What isn't or can't be used travels via the bloodstream to the last part of the loop, the liver. The job of the liver is to break down or bond hormones together to inactivate them and eliminate them from the body in stool and urine. When production, utilization, and elimination work normally, there are no symptoms.

If a woman has a hormonal problem or imbalance—we can call it PMS or menopausal symptoms or any other name we want to apply—it means there is some sort of disregulation in one or sometimes multiple points in the loop. It is a complex process and questionable whether it is wise to add chemical hormones through replacement therapy or recommend any other kind of treatment before discovering where on this loop the problem occurs or if, indeed, the source of the problem is hormonally based.

The problem could be in the area of hormone production. For any number of reasons—deficiencies in minerals or essential fatty acids, not enough or too many hormones being produced, and so on—the body may be unable to make the hormones it needs. Or perhaps the problem is with hormone utilization. For the body to be balanced, estrogen and progesterone have to be picked up by estrogen and progesterone receptors. Sometimes there are too few or too many receptors. Sometimes the receptors are blocked and can't bind with the hormone, and the body *appears* to be hormonally imbalanced. We have to figure out if it is truly a hormonal imbalance or whether something else is blocking the receptors. Synthetic chemicals and compounds, including prescriptive and nonprescriptive drugs, may also interfere with the body's normal functioning. Common substances present in many foods we eat, like preservatives, colorings, pesticides, and the like, may act to destabilize the body. Estrogen and progesterone, too, could be blocked, never reaching the cells designed to receive them. This is basic biochemistry, but few study the effects of drugs or preservatives or food colorings in the system and their impact on cell function.

In fact, a hormonal imbalance could already exist even before menopause. And when the natural production of hormones begins to diminish, adding synthetic hormones could further complicate the body's functioning. It is very hard to measure the origins of these imbalances without doing some elaborate and extensive studies of receptor sites. These are seldom done; generally it is assumed that replacing estrogen and progesterone synthetically will override the imbalances.

All the hormones we produce must eventually be degraded and broken down (detoxified) by the liver. Understand, however, that the capacity of the liver to detoxify is finite. If it is too busy breaking down all the processed, preserved, chemically laden foods we eat, it will hardly operate at optimum. And other compounds may not be adequately broken down or degraded. If estrogen is not broken down, it may float around in active form. Synthetic estradiol is the compound used in the estrogen skin patch—it delivers estrogen directly into the bloodstream when applied to the skin—and its purpose, like the natural hormone it simulates, is to act as a cell proliferant, causing cells to multiply. If hormones are floating around in larger than desired amounts, other cells in the estrogen-sensitive tissues and organs may multiply and cause further problems in the body, such as endometriosis, fibroids, and breast cysts.

This, too, is standard biochemistry, and I don't know why this information is not made available to women before hormone replacement therapy is prescribed. If we are going to add hormones from an outside source, we have to ask, What other parts of the system are involved, and at what level are they functioning? Can the liver handle more hormones? This does not imply liver disease, by the way. You could have a liver that is overwhelmed and can't handle all its responsibilities and still show no medical sign of "disease."

The liver gets rid of hormones primarily via the bowel and urinary tract, by converting them into what are called "conjugated" or inactive forms. However, if the bowel bacteria is not correct—not optimized—certain bacteria can deconjugate the estrogen and reactivate it in the bowel. So if a woman has chronic constipation, the hormone that should be eliminated may instead remain in the bowel long enough to be reactivated, allowing it to be reabsorbed into the bloodstream.

This resorption on a regular basis can cause a hormonal body imbalance, creating what seem to be menopausal symptoms—hot flashes, depression, and the like. Deactivation capacity in the liver and elimination through urine and stool is an important component in the regulation loop. When the body and ultimately the cells are properly nourished and therefore functioning properly, the feedback loop should self-correct, and menopause can be a relatively symptomless passage.

A reason why one woman may experience more intense symptoms than another involves the issue of "constitution." A woman with a "delicate" system or constitution might feel things more dramatically than another with a more "robust" makeup. Some women with severe symptoms respond very well to treatment, if the causes are fairly superficial. Other cases with fairly moderate symptoms can have deep-seated origins, and it could take a lot longer to alleviate them. But if a woman absolutely needed estrogen or progesterone from an outside source to diminish symptoms, natural forms of both these hormones are available, usually derived from the wild Mexican yam (see Dr. Corsello, page 22).

There used to be some rules of thumb by which we could approximate the amount of time it would take to reverse a condition by knowing how many years someone had experienced a problem. But, in general, the more chronic the case—the more interventions, the more drugs taken—the more difficult it is to alleviate the condition and the more time it takes.

There is a great deal a woman can do for herself to begin the sometimes very long process of balancing her body. She can work to improve her digestion by eating plenty of fresh vegetables and whole-grain fiber—cereals, breads, pasta, and so on—drinking adequate amounts of water, and reducing her meat consumption. That can go a long way toward helping with problems like constipation.

I find that for most people, knowledge becomes the key motivator for change. Knowing only that sugar causes tooth decay is not a very powerful motivator to stop eating sweets. But if you know that sugar also depletes B_6 and zinc and can significantly impair your immune response and cause a whole host of metabolic disturbances, you have a much more powerful motivation for change. You may like sweets, but if for twenty minutes of enjoyment you have to pay with many days of feeling terrible, it just isn't worth it. And when people are aware of the equation, it becomes easier not to indulge.

Eating fats, for example, is considered by most people to be unhealthy. But if you know that when you eat fats it takes a very long time for your body to eliminate them—the half-life of fatty acids in the body is about two years—and that there are both good and bad fats, the awareness can make a substantial difference in what you choose to eat.

Knowing the difference between good fats and bad fats can help us make better decisions. Too many people have poor-quality fats in their tissues—mainly the saturated ones and trans-fatty acids—from years of margarine use, years of fried foods, years of otherwise scorched and oxidized oils that the body has had to deal with. Trans-fatty acids, the manmade semisaturated hydrogenated oils, are as undesirable as the fats in meats and animal products—all are potential carcinogens. And if you ingest too many of these fats, you may need to do an oil change to achieve a healthier fatty-acid balance. Dry hair, dry eyes, and dry skin can all be symptoms of a deficiency of good-quality fatty acids.

So the "good fats" can be used to our advantage. We can change the whole architecture of the fatty structures in our bodies by shifting the balance to positive fats. There are two main categories of "good fats":

1. The omega-6 fatty acids, which include linoleic acid (the most essential of the fatty acids), found in nuts, wheat germ, and vegetable oils. Primrose oil or borage oil have large amounts of linoleic acid, as well as a special fatty acid called GLA, which is used therapeutically to enhance the production of certain prostaglandins—tissue hormones—in the body that influence inflammation, water balance, immune response, and more.

2. The omega-3 oils, typically found in fish oils—salmon and mackerel particularly. These fatty acids are the source for specific prostaglandins. Unfortunately, people don't eat much of the fatty fish anymore, perhaps because they think all fat is bad. Or if they do eat them, the fish oils may be damaged by high-temperature frying or oxidation. Fats, oils, and the foods that contain them should be handled gently and stored properly.

Changing the way we eat is totally within our reach. If we are to be healthy, we need to learn which are real foods and which are pseudofoods—the ones that look, taste, and smell like real foods but have no nutritional value—because what we decide to eat today will determine the quality of the brain cells, nerve cells, and uterine cells of tomorrow, like it or not.

I also want to emphasize that ingesting a nutrient—any nutrient—does not necessarily mean you are absorbing it. The nutrients have to be absorbed and then transported to the tissues and organs. The cells are what must be nourished. If the nutrients are not absorbed, they simply come out in the stool. Some people may be taking vitamins and minerals with the very best intentions, but their cells could still be starved, creating any number of problems in the body that need therapeutic attention.

As we get older, we may also find that we don't digest certain foods as we used to when we were younger. Our ability to handle concentrated proteins like meat tends to decrease with age because stomach acid production lessens after age thirty-five. But I don't think everyone needs to be a vegetarian. Again, the "one size fits all" approach to health, and especially diet, doesn't work because people have individual problems. Some people do well with a modest level of animal protein in their diet. Using natural meats every two weeks—free of antibiotics—should present no real problem to them, but remember: these are guidelines for the healthy.

Fifty or even 60 percent of the diet should be vegetable based: lightly cooked, steamed, or stir-fried vegetables and whole grains—whole wheat, rice, oats, and barley. Then come legumes—lentils, kidney beans, chick peas—which provide you with a source of nonanimal protein. Fruits are also important, taken primarily in season; if possible, they should be relatively indigenous to your area. Modest animal protein or animal products like milk or eggs may be appropriate as well. Fat intake should be limited. People have mistakenly been told that nuts and seeds are fattening, but they are tremendous powerhouses of minerals, magnesium, and zinc. Almonds are a wonderful source of calcium, along with sunflower seeds, and the fats in them are desirable, if the nuts are not roasted or otherwise abused. I also recommend drinking at least three sixteen-ounce glasses of water per day between meals (not with meals), in addition to any juice or other beverages you drink.

Fresh food is always preferred, provided it's of reasonable quality; frozen is second, and canned is really like buying leftovers. But organically raised vegetables and fruits have a much higher mineral content compared with those that are commercially raised. When you artificially fertilize crops, the plants don't take up the amount of zinc or manganese or magnesium from the soil that they can with natural fertilizers. In many cases commercial farmland has been overfarmed for 150 years, with no replenishment of the nutrient base our bodies need. So eating a wonderfully fresh, locally picked food supply still doesn't guarantee that our nutrient needs will be met.

I don't think it ever was true—and certainly it's not true today—that simply having a good diet will provide you with what you need for optimal health. Most studies that have been done around the world on different populations show that people's intake of nutrients is never ideal; they have an overabundance of some nutrients and a deficit of one or more other nutrients. But what kind and how much supplementation may be required is an individual matter. Someone who has been eating right from day one may need only simple supplementation compared with a woman of forty-five who is only now beginning to eat properly after thirty-five years of dietary abuse. Starting a wonderful, healthful eating pattern today is terrific but will not atone for the indulgent years or restore lost reserves.

Having said that, I will state that vitamin C is universally needed. It is a wonderful antioxidant. With 2000 mg a day you're getting some protection against the accumulation of heavy metals like lead, mercury, cadmium, and possibly aluminum. Everyone can use a good multivitamin that's well manufactured and easily absorbed and provides between 30 and 50 mg of the B vitamins.

The emphasis on calcium has to be put into perspective. Calcium is important, of course, but not any more so than magnesium, manganese, boron, copper, and zinc, along with the vitamin C it takes to make bones—a living protein matrix—into which the body deposits many minerals. That deposition process is controlled by a complex system, including thyroid, parathyroid, tissue pH, and a dozen other factors. If the physiology is out of balance or nutrients are deficient, any supplemented calcium may be of questionable benefit. With a calcium regulation problem, additional calcium may lead only to calcification of soft tissues, causing calcium deposits where they shouldn't be—in the joints or possibly in breast tissue. Calcium deposits can develop anywhere in the body, not just in bone.

Osteoporosis is the result of the demineralization process, common in Westernized people. Not only do we lack minerals in the foods we eat, but because our diets are overly acidic and have been for years, our bodies have also become increasingly acidic, causing minerals to be leached out of our cells and tissues. People need to eat more alkaline foods to offset the effects of excess acidity. A therapeutic nutritional program may include 80 percent alkalinizing foods and 20 percent acidic foods to bring the body closer to optimal pH, or balance. Examples of high acidic foods are beer, ice cream, sugar, fried foods, and even natural soy beans. Medium-acidic foods are pork, veal, and chicken. Very alkaline foods include pumpkin seeds, yams, lentils, nectarines, watermelon, and tangerines. Some foods like lemons, for example, are acidic in taste but create an alkaline effect in the body. Charts and tables listing the acid/alkaline effects of foods are available to assist in structuring diets.

But again, it is not a matter of avoiding acid foods or concentrating on alkaline foods. We have to work for balance. If we have negative conditions in the body, we have to do certain things to get well. When we are well, the balance changes and we have to move from therapy to maintenance. But the balance is different for different people, and most people need a clinician to help guide them when measuring the acid/base balance.

I think the first thing for a woman to do, especially at menopause, when she approaches alternative therapies is to become familiar with the concepts, ideas, and philosophies of the various healing systems available to her. Most of us accept and utilize what we are familiar with, not because it's safe or the best way, but because it's known. We fear, or at least shy away from, the unknown. From a practitioner's viewpoint, the more a client understands the limitations and benefits of different modalities, the easier it is for the client to see why one may work better for her than another. But it is her decision. I may think in a particular case that nutritional therapy is the best long-term way to go, but if she wants to go with something she understands better—for example, herbals—she has the option to pursue that to its greatest effectiveness. Maybe it is 40 percent or even 80 percent effective. But once she has achieved some success with one modality, then perhaps she'll be ready to go farther, with homeopathy or something else. With an open, inquiring mind, thoughtful analysis, and competent guidance, most people can be pleasantly surprised by what the human system can achieve! The fundamental question is whether we are going to assist nature and the natural process of healing or fight against the body and its efforts to self-regulate. The choice is ours.

Twelve Principles for Healthy Eating

These twelve basic principles for healthy eating are compatible with Dr. Sullender's thinking and also sum up many other expert approaches to diet and nutrition to be followed, not only at menopause, but during the years beyond.

Most of us eat twenty-one meals, more or less, every week. If we break the rules during a few of those meals, it's hardly catastrophic. But try not to skip meals, particularly breakfast, because you are breaking a fast of as much as twelve hours. You need food.

1. Eat lots of fresh vegetables, particularly dark green and leafy—cooked and raw. Eat plenty of salads and particularly brussels sprouts, broccoli, cabbage, kale, and collard greens. You can eat very well on a varied diet of vegetables.
2. Eat fruit, all kinds.
3. Eat whole-grain breads, cereals, grains (brown rice is always good), and pasta, always in preference to processed bread and white rice.
4. If you eat dairy products, do it rarely (eggs, cheese, yogurt, cottage cheese, milk, and cream), and when you do make sure they're low-fat. If you drink milk, drink skim. Seaweed—or sea vegetables, as macrobiotics call the different varieties they use—is very high in calcium. Sprinkle it on salads and eat it regularly if you are a vegetarian.
5. If you eat red meat, eat very, very little and if possible eat meat from animals who are fed chemical- and hormone-free feed. Try three ounces a couple of times a week, stir fried with very little oil and mixed with vegetables. This is a good way to get animal protein. Eat fish and chicken without the skin, but again, eat small portions and only a few times a week. Salmon, mackerel, and other fatty fish are great for lowering cholesterol. Natural tofu is a valuable vegetable protein food. It can be sautéed, steamed, or eaten uncooked and served cold over hot brown rice with toasted sesame seeds and tamari sauce—a natural soy product.
6. Eat beans, peas, and lentils, well cooked. Soups are a great way to use dried legumes.
7. Don't use butter, margarine, and other hydrogenated fats. But if you can't eat toast without butter, use it sparingly.

Substitute almond oil or olive oil, but be sensible: high-fat foods are regarded as unhealthy by all diet experts and unacceptable by others, but what constitutes "high fat" is controversial.

8. Fried foods of any kind, along with cakes, pies, cookies, and rich desserts, should be eaten only occasionally. The combination of fats and sugar are lethal. Choose desserts made with natural fruit for sweetness. But enjoy all desserts only every once in a while and keep them out of your daily diet.

9. Watch any added sugar and salt; do without if you can.

10. Keep alcohol, coffee, and tea to a minimum. A glass of wine, for a special occasion, a cup of coffee or tea a day, probably won't hurt you. However, as reported in *The New York Times,* "Dr. Matthew Longnecker of the University of California at Los Angeles analyzed 38 studies on alcohol and breast cancer. He concluded that one drink a day increased breast cancer risk by about 10 percent and two drinks increased it by 25 percent."

11. Try not to eat between meals, if you eat three meals a day. Or try eating five tiny meals to keep from getting hungry.

12. Drink eight to ten eight-ounce glasses of water a day.

Healers

In the world of alternative medicine, the designation of "healer" is given to one who has abilities that extend beyond the five senses. Perhaps he or she has highly attuned intuitive abilities, sometimes metaphysical knowledge that helps in diagnosis and treatment. Some healers see auras—the emanation of different levels of energy given off from all living things—and understand how to interpret the colors and the intensity of light relative to the state of a patient's health. Some can work to change the energy fields in the body through their hands. Others have psychic abilities that give them information about the probable causes of physical problems. That kind of ability can be useful when the cause can't be determined by medical tests.

The recent explosion of interest in metaphysical realities, quantum physics, space and time travel, and all kinds of science fiction has stirred great interest in metaphysics, but it has also tended to romanticize abilities we do not understand. In all probability, each of us has some of these skills, but we simply have not developed them. And I am certain that no single person can effect an instant miracle cure for any physical condition—normal aches and pains, chronic illness, or serious disease states—even if it appears that way. But I am equally sure that there are people who can help us tap into the body's ability to heal itself, hastening the process back to a balance of mind and body.

Interview with a Healer

Several years ago I was introduced to a healer whose work has encouraged me to broaden my ideas about the possibilities of alternative medicine. She is both teacher and health practitioner. Her approach to healing differs from individual to individual, and she responds to their immediate needs while working to improve the whole body at the same time. She specializes in herb and vitamin treatment and does hands-on body work to lessen stress and balance the body by moving the energy held in the various muscles, tendons, and organs. Her deep knowledge comes through years of independent study and practical experience. She works as a private consultant on a referral only basis.

This remarkable woman agreed to be interviewed on the subject of a general program appropriate for use by any healthy woman in menopause, but she asked that her name not be included in the book. She said, "The herbs and folk remedies I tell you about are traditional. It is not privileged information. People working in the field suggest them regularly, but when you recommend dosages as well, it can be considered prescribing, even if the purpose is to rebalance the body rather than cure an illness. I want your readers to remember that these are general remedies and that if they try any of them, they are prescribing for themselves and are accepting the responsibility for the results." She also tells her clients to let their doctors know they are using supplements.

A General Health Program for Women in Menopause

In menopause, as the estrogen level decreases, so does the calcium level. Calcium is necessary to build the outer bone structure, but you can't stop there—chromium and selenium build the inner structure. That's why taking calcium alone isn't effective in lessening osteoporosis. But replacing the chromium and selenium is tricky. I agree with doctors who tell you not to take chromium and selenium pills unless you know what you're doing because you can overthicken or thin down the inner bone. That's why I suggest going with alfalfa and kelp; they carry chromium and selenium in a less intense form.

To Sustain Bones Naturally

Morning and night:

500 mg calcium (builds outer bones)

3 alfalfa pills (provides chromium and selenium)

3 kelp pills (provides chromium and selenium)

To Lift Estrogen Level Lightly

Morning and night:

1 black cohosh capsule

Relaxation and Removal of Toxins from the Body

Twice a week:

Apple cider vinegar bath

Directions: Start bathwater, then add 1 cup of natural apple cider vinegar. Get in, and continue filling tub with water as hot as you can stand it. Stay in until water cools down. If you get dizzy at any time, get out of the tub.

Promote Circulation/Lessen Hot Flashes

Once or twice a week:

Baking Soda Bath

Directions: Start bathwater, then add 1 cup of baking soda. Get in and fill tub with water as hot as you can stand it. Stay in the bath until the water cools down. If you get dizzy at any time, get out of the tub.

Vaginal Dryness

Take 1 black cohosh twice a day. If this does not relieve the condition, increase the dosage to 2 or 3 capsules in the morning and 2 in the evening for a week to 2 weeks. Then reduce to 2 in the morning and 1 at night. Finally, reduce back to 1 in the morning and 1 at night.

White vinegar (with water) douche:
This cleans as well as stimulates the walls of the vagina. The vagina can hold old secretions for months, and that's irritating to the tissues.

Daily:

1000 mg vitamin A
1000 mg vitamin D
1000 mg vitamin E

Liquid forms of vitamins A, D, and E can also be applied with your fingers to the inside of the vagina for extra moisture.

Heavy Bleeding

This condition is usually caused by a buildup of blood that is not draining properly. There are three possible treatments.

Treatment 1:
Mistletoe in capsule form
Take 1 capsule in the morning and 1 at night starting approximately 4 or 5 days before expecting a period. Stop taking it as soon as the period ends.

Mistletoe should decrease the bleeding and make a woman more comfortable. This herb helps clean out the uterus, so the next period is less heavy. Don't take more without consulting an herbalist, because mistletoe can stop not only the hemorrhaging, but the periods altogether.

Treatment 2:
White Oak Bark in capsule form
Take 1 capsule in the morning and 1 at night starting approximately 4 or 5 days before expecting a period. Stop taking it as soon as the period ends.

Treatment 3:
Cayenne in capsule form
Take 1 capsule in the morning and 1 at night starting approximately 4 or 5 days before expecting a period. Stop taking it as soon as the period ends. Cayenne tends to affect the stomach. How-

ever, if you are used to eating highly spiced foods regularly as part of your diet, cayenne can be used successfully to decrease heavy bleeding.

Heavy Bleeding with Cramping

Treatment:

Dong Quai in capsule form

Dong quai is effective in decreasing blood flow but works particularly well when there is cramping during a heavy period. Take 1 capsule in the morning and 1 at night starting approximately 4 or 5 days before expecting a period. Stop taking it as soon as the period ends.

Heavy Bleeding with an Infection

Treatment:

Golden Seal and Mistletoe

Take 1 capsule of golden seal in the morning and 1 at night along with 1 capsule of mistletoe morning and night starting approximately 4 or 5 days before expecting a period. Stop taking the mistletoe as soon as the period ends. Continue taking the golden seal in the morning and night through the next period or until the odor disappears, indicating that the infection has been eliminated.

Exceptionally Heavy Bleeding

If exceptionally heavy bleeding continues over several months or there is sudden heavy bleeding, a woman should consult her gynecologist to make sure there is no abnormal reason for the bleeding.

Hot Flashes

A number of herbs can be used to quiet hot flashes. One may work better for you than another, so if you get no relief after a month or 6 weeks, try a different herb. The herbs begin to take effect immediately, but you may not notice the difference for as long as 30 days. You could, of course, speed up the results by increasing the dosage, but if the changes happen in your body too quickly, there could be an emotional imbalance.

Treatment 1:
Dong Quai in capsule form
Take 1 capsule in the morning and 1 at night.

Treatment 2:
Damiana in capsule form
Take 1 capsule in the morning and 1 at night.

You might also try taking black cohosh in capsule form along with any of the above hot flash herbs. Start with the minimum dose: 1 capsule in the morning and 1 at night, particularly if you are still menstruating.

If you have stopped menstruating, you can increase the dosage of black cohosh up to 4 a day, but no more. Cut back to the minimum dose when the hot flashes subside.

Extreme Hot Flashes with Emotional Stress

Ninety percent of the time, severe hot flashes are the result of an emotional tie-up. Women get to the place where they don't understand the changes going on in their bodies and how it exacerbates their attitudes and feelings. For the kinds of hot flashes that make even normal stress difficult to handle, try valerian. Herbs like valerian have been around for thousands of years, but only recently have they been made available in easy-to-use forms. The herb comes in both pill and liquid form, but the tinctures are easier to use. Valerian is commonly taken for emotional stress; it acts like Valium but has no side effects, although a small percentage of women can become irritable and restless.

The key to using valerian is determining your tolerance for the herb. Every person responds differently to herbs, so start lightly and increase the dosage slowly until the problem is relieved. The right dosage for you brings your body to a balanced state; you can function normally both mentally and physically.

Treatment:

3 or 4 drops of valerian (a light dose) in a glass of water or juice to quiet one's mind and lighten hot flashes. Use as needed.

Valerian generally works in less than 20 minutes, but if there is little or no relief, wait an hour and take 3 or 4 more drops.

Improving Circulation to Calm Hot Flashes

Hot flashes are intensified by poor blood circulation. A hiatal hernia can sometimes be the problem. Some serious hiatal hernias need medical attention, while others (known as "subclinical hernias") produce a similar condition but do not show up in clinical tests as hiatal hernias. Subclinical hernias can be relieved easily without drugs.

When you eat, your food is carried by a long tube called the *esophagus* to the stomach. The food travels down this tube and makes its way through the diaphraghm, a partition of muscles and tendons that separate the chest cavity from the abdominal cavity. At the end of the esophagus is a muscular valve called the *lower esophagal sphincter (LES)*. The LES opens when triggered by food and closes after the food is passed into the esophagal hiatas—the lower part of the esophagus—which leads to the stomach, where digestion takes place.

If the mechanism is not working normally (you eat too fast or too much or are under stress), the valve opens to let food in but fails to close properly, allowing the stomach acids to push back up through the esophagus. But more problematic than that, part of the stomach itself can protrude into the hiatus. Technically, a subclinical hernia is not a hernia, because there is no rupture. But it is abnormal for food to stagnate above the diaphragm; the gases that are created end up swelling and physically displacing the esophagal wall.

This condition pressures other organs and affects circulation throughout the body and can result in many negative body conditions; hot flashes are only one of them. Good blood circulation is critical to health, particularly as we get older.

Recommended Exercise

Directions: Perform this exercise 4 times a day: when you wake up in the morning, before lunch, before dinner, and before going to sleep.

Step 1: Lie flat on your back with your knees raised and feet flat on the floor. Relax.

Step 2: Make a fist with one hand, keeping your thumb inside.

Step 3: Place your fist just beneath the breastbone, right at the "V" where your ribs meet.

Step 4: Place your other hand on top of your fist for added pressure.

Step 5: Take a deep breath, and on the exhale, rotate your fist downward toward your belly button.
Do this 3 times, making sure to breathe.

Burning Sensation in the Urethra

Dryness, caused by the decreasing production of oils, often means there is too much acid in the body. Hormone imbalances during menopause can also add to the discomfort.

Treatment:

Baking soda baths (see page 127).
1 black cohosh in the morning,
1 black cohosh at night.

Liver Spots

Poor nutrients, lack of circulation, lack of oils, and improper function of the liver all contribute to the formation of liver spots.

Treatment:

Try applying lemon juice directly on the skin.
Try barberry or angelica in a low dose.
(1 morning, 1 night) for 3 months and see if there is improvement.

Bladder Weakness

Treatment:

1 buchu (see page 203) in the morning and 1 at night.

It may take about 45 days before buchu begins to work. If the leakage is mild, it could work faster.

3 Calc. Fluor. (calcium fluoride) #1 cell salts morning and night (see page 218).

Hair Loss

Treatment:

Black cohosh, 1 in the morning and 1 at night.

3 silica pills 4 times a day (#12 Silica is a cell salt—a homeopathic remedy).

Part Three

Women Who Manage Menopause Naturally

Women have hard knowledge in the area of health," Dr. Loretta Mears said during our interview. "It's bred from the experience of caregiving."

I was struck by the truth of her words when I listened to the women I interviewed. They come from a variety of different backgrounds, but they share the knowledge and experience gained by managing menopause without estrogen. They talked openly about what happens, how it feels, and they tell us what they do in their comprehensive programs. Five are married, four are single, and one is widowed. All but one of them—and she is over eighty years old—have active jobs and careers. They represent all of us who want to make this transition as comfortably as we can and want to maintain the energy levels and stamina we have been able to take for granted before menopause.

One of the main reasons for including these women's experiences is to demystify the process of handling menopause naturally. However, each woman tailored her program to meet specific needs and goals. Some wanted only to eliminate menopausal symptoms without hormones. Others sought to prevent osteoporosis and other diseases. And some women embraced menopause as an opportunity—a time to pay closer attention to their health because their hormone levels were changing.

Whether you use them to treat symptoms or prevent disease, alternative therapies require that practitioner and patient work together to find the best solution to the problem. A gradual improvement in health is one of the realities of alternative medicine, and to expect instant changes is to invite disappointment and disillusionment.

Most of the women I interviewed chose to work with alternative specialists as well as their gynecologists, and they do not seem to find the two approaches to health care incompatible despite their differences.

I do not pretend in any way that this small sample of women is scientific. I don't know how many women are getting through menopause with alternative treatments, but I can tell you it was not difficult to find women who are doing just that. It was, however, more difficult to find women who were on complete programs, who understood that exercise, a proper diet, and taking herbs and vitamins all play a significant part in keeping us healthy as we age. I included the stories of two women who are not on specific programs. One woman used a vitamin compound regimen that worked so quickly for her, I felt it was worthwhile for other women to know about it. The other woman uses homeopathic remedies, but presently she is not on a regular program of diet and exercise.

I hesitated to include the herb and vitamin regimens these women follow because the supplements and dosages differ, even though the symptoms are similar. But that may be the point of including them in such detail: alternative medicine is very personal, and what works for one woman may not work for another. I take their word that the herbs they use work, that the vitamins they take are effective for them, and it is interesting for me to note the similarities as well as the differences.

Almost all of the women I interviewed used vitamin E in pill or liquid form and took calcium and vitamin C. Half of them took a multivitamin every day, and the same number used some homeopathic remedies. Two of the women took an over-the-counter natural herb and vitamin compound for hot flashes. Four of the women used ginseng for hot flashes, and three took a glandular tablet of raw adrenal (see page 221) to raise their energy levels. Most of them pay attention to their diets and exercise regularly.

These women have lots of advice for the rest of us based on personal experience—what works and what doesn't. They also have suggestions for finding practitioners and selecting herbs and vitamins, and they give us their programs. In reading their stories, we learn how they are getting through menopause, establishing patterns that will keep their bodies balanced as they grow older, and we get some idea of how we might do it, too.

Alisyn

Choosing Menopause Without Estrogen

Alisyn is a fifty-four-year-old writer whose interest in alternative medicine began ten years ago when she sought treatment to avoid surgery for very large fibroid tumors. There was some evidence that the herbs she was taking were shrinking the fibroids, but her anxiety—fed by the gynecologist's concern that the tumors might be cancerous—led to her decision to have a partial hysterectomy. The fibroids were benign, as most fibroids are (only .5 percent are malignant), and Alisyn was able to keep her ovaries.

"With my fibroids taken care of," she says, "I began to think about alternative therapies as preventive medicine rather than as curative medicine. I realized that I had been so concerned about getting rid of the fibroids that I'd missed the philosophical core of natural health: balancing mind and body, emotionally and physically, to help prevent the development of serious illness."

When her hormone levels diminished at about age fifty, Alisyn had already decided not to take estrogen. She says:

I'd been on a vitamin and herb program for several years before the signs of menopause were unmistakable—hot when everyone else was cold, vaginal dryness, some mood swings. My gynecologist wanted me to take estrogen, and I told him I'd think about it, although I had really made up my mind that I was going to pass. But he wrote me a prescription for an estrogen cream for my vaginal dryness, anyway. I tried it for about a week as prescribed, but my vagina felt as if it were tingling—very uncomfortable—so I stopped using it. K-Y jelly combined with liquid Vitamin E works fine. If I need the estrogen cream in the future, I'll use a "less is more" approach. I read somewhere that it really doesn't take much to bring back the tissues; I mean, even one-eighth the dosage can work. And when combined with a lubricant like Vitamin E, it's effective for relieving painful intercourse. But they warn against using estrogen cream as a lubricant. It's medicine and should be used sparingly.

At that time I decided to talk with my herbal specialist; she had seen me through colds and skin problems and various aches and pains, so I was sure she would help me get through menopause. And she did, by putting me on a program that's really worked. I haven't had any symptoms for several years now. She designed the program for me; most good herbalists do that. She combined herbs and vitamins to take care of the symptoms, but she also told me what I needed to do—exercise, have massage, and make some changes in my diet—to counteract stress. I had been a vegetarian, and she suggested I include a few ounces of animal protein a week—not only chicken or fish, but beef, too. I have to admit I don't like red meat, so I only eat it mixed with vegetables, if I eat it at all. The program also includes homeopathic and folk remedies to help my general health.

At first it all seemed too folksy to be taken seriously—like drinking lemon juice and honey in hot water every morning for regularity (which works, by the way). We're so used to high-concept packaging and being suspicious of anything that isn't prescribed by the doctor that we forget the simple treatments that work for common health problems. My medicine cabinet has been cleared of over-the-counter drugs and replaced with things like apple cider vinegar for baths, castor oil—it's odorless these days—used with a heating pad for colds and aches and pains. I also keep dry mustard to make mustard plasters for bronchial problems. And of course there's the bottle of white vinegar for douching. It's amazing to me that manufacturers are bottling white vinegar and water in a package and selling it for four times the cost of buying the vinegar and doing it yourself. You wait and see, when herbs and vitamins become mainstream, corporations will begin packaging, bottling, advertising, and marketing all the odd things I'm putting together myself now.

By the way, my herbalist is not at all against estrogen replacement therapy. She says that if women are very stressed, they may need the stronger synthetic estrogen, but they should have the option to use both estrogen and herbs at the same time, and then drop the estrogen to see whether the herbs are doing the job.

I also have to tell you about something called Bach Rescue Remedy. It was recommended by another herbalist I met when I was undergoing a period of intense work with short deadlines. I was very anxious and overwrought, and Rescue Remedy is aptly named—it literally rescued me, calmed me down, allowed me to focus and keep working. It was so remarkable that after my crisis I actually did research on Dr. Edward Bach and discovered that he was a British doctor who developed a unique form of homeopathy called the Bach Flower Remedies. There are thirty-eight remedies that relieve thirty-eight different emotional and mental states. *Handbook of the Bach Flower Remedies*[11] has a chapter on each of the thirty-eight remedies. Among them are the five included in Rescue Remedy: star of Bethlehem for shock; rock rose for terror and panic; impatiens for mental stress and tension; cherry plum for desperation; and clematis for the bemused, faraway, out-of-the-body feeling that often precedes fainting or loss of consciousness. It is fascinating to me that these remedies have been available since the 1930s and that I just learned about them this year. The idea that someone developed a natural treatment for emotional and mental states that have no side effects and that everyone is not running to the health food store to buy them amazes me.

Besides herbs and vitamins and flower remedies, I'm very interested in the mind/body therapies that are available today. The West Coast is so far ahead of us here on the East Coast. I've begun to understand how stress affects me, how much tension I build up in my neck and shoulders and back. I actually didn't know what it felt like not to be tight. Even when I thought I was relaxing, I was tense. Working on a computer every day and sitting in one position doesn't help the situation. A massage every week isn't a luxury anymore.

In addition to the masseuse, I use all kinds of alternative therapists regularly. My acupuncturist has helped loosen a tight shoulder that wasn't helped by massage. I've had reflexology done on my feet, although I've never used it therapeutically. It is hard to believe that someone can actually work on my feet for an hour and that it really relaxes my whole body. I usually see a chiropractor to adjust my spine several times a year. She also functions as my GP, checks my blood pressure and so forth. The last time I went to her, I'd been clenching my jaw and grinding my teeth, so she just reached in my mouth and released the jaw, and it's been fine since then. What's great about seeing these therapists is that I go to them basically healthy, knowing they can take care of the minor problems and help me to be even healthier. Unlike when I go to the doctor, I never feel anxious about the appointment. I think my experience with alternative healers has made me braver about dealing with a doctor's disapproval. They don't know everything, and that's okay with me. When I see them, I want their best information, but I don't need their uninformed opinions on therapies they have not studied.

I still have a gynecologist and an internist, but I can imagine a time when I won't need them.

Alisyn's Program

Morning and night:

1 black cohosh capsule (to raise estrogen level)
1 raw adrenal (to increase energy)
1 Siberian ginseng (to increase energy)
3 #7 Kali. Sulph. cell salts (potassium sulphate)
3 #9 Nat. Mur. cell salts (sodium chloride)
4 #4 Ferr. Phos. (iron phosphate)
250 mg B_{12} (The combination of Ferr. Phos. and B_{12} fills iron requirement.)
500 mg vitamin C
500 mg calcium
10 drops liquid mullein (for sinus problems)

Diet

Primarily vegetables, fruits, and grains
3 ounces chicken, fish, or meat 3 times a week
A snack-size box of raisins for supplementary iron 3 times a week

Exercise

Light exercise (walking regularly)
More strenuous exercise (2 hours a week of Pilates; see page 75)

Massage

Regular massage (to relieve tension and improve circulation)

Minor stress

In addition to the Bach Flower Remedies I often use valerian for minor stress. I dissolve five to seven drops of valerian root in some water or juice. It works like a tranquilizer, but it doesn't interfere with concentration or make me sleepy. But when I've had the occasional bout of insomnia, I've taken from ten to fifteen drops—that dosage always relaxes me enough to sleep.

Connie

Vitamins, Minerals, Herbs, and Exercise

Connie is a fifty-two-year-old vitamin consultant who works for a midtown New York health food store. She has been married for twenty-six years and has two grown sons. In 1988, at age forty-seven, Connie had a radical hysterectomy for cervical cancer; it was a very aggressive type of cancer, and after the operation her doctor recommended a course of chemotherapy. As a long-time vegetarian, runner, and natural health advocate, Connie was against taking powerful chemicals into her body and she began to look for alternatives to chemo and, concurrently, estrogen for the hot flashes that developed immediately after the surgery.

"I read everything I could get my hands on—books, newspaper and magazine articles, pamphlets from herb and vitamin suppliers. There were two books I found particularly useful and still use all the time: *Everywoman's Book*[12] and *Prescription for Nutritional Healing.*"[13]

Connie's research convinced her that she needed to strengthen her immune system. She began a program that made her feel better almost immediately and lessened her hot flashes. She has had no recurrence of the cancer and continues on the same high-dose vitamin and mineral program, along with maintaining a regular exercise schedule. Connie tells us:

I think the most important thing you can do for yourself at this age to prevent disease is to keep your circulation going. I began running six days a week. I try to do at least three miles. I bike and I row.

In terms of the self-prescription I do, I take lecithin to keep my arteries supple and to keep the blood pumping through them normally. Lecithin also decreases some of the irritating symptoms of menopause like hot flashes, vaginal dryness, and memory loss. The choline in lecithin—lecithin is the B vitamin made up of inositol and choline—brought my memory back. Once you lose natural estrogen, there's a change in the thought synapses to the brain. The B vitamins help my short-term memory and my concentration.

Even though my body was changing after menopause, my life-style didn't change. I was busier than ever, and to make sure I could do everything I wanted, I started to take Siberian ginseng, which has estrogenic components. It has helped me a great deal. In *Love, Sex and Nutrition,* Dr. Bernard Jensen suggests that Siberian ginseng is a good balancing herb, one that doesn't keep you awake at night, and is the best kind of ginseng for women.

When my family and I began taking vitamins we didn't know very much about them—we bought inexpensive brands. But a friend told me about Shaklee vitamins, and my family all started taking them. I saw a big, big difference. I lost weight, my energy level went up. The difference between synthetic vitamins and natural ones is the rate of absorption. Doctors will tell you there is no difference between them, but I see the results in my body. Natural vitamins are really worth the money. But, be careful: a vitamin can be labeled "natural" with only thirty percent of the natural element—you have to learn to read the fine print on the back of the bottle. In general, a natural vitamin costs more than the synthetic. Take vitamin C. You can get it for a dollar a bottle, but the formulation will be a chemical equivalent rather than an authentic version made from plant extracts. I've had customers come into the store who have broken out in a rash from taking synthetic rather than natural vitamins. One woman reacted with bruises all over her body. The chemicals act as antagonists, and the body has to work very hard to break them down. You're lucky if you absorb half the synthetic vitamins you take. Because of this it's very important to read labels so you know what you're taking. Also make sure that any vitamin you take is not encased in bovine gel. Natural vegetarian gel caps break down in your body much faster.

The Shaklee brand is very good. I trust the quality. These vitamins break down in water instantaneously, which means they do the same thing in the body. I don't sell them, by the way—they're only available through representatives—I just use them. The Solgar brand is excellent, too. Solgar makes an earth source vitamin that has wheat-grass and spirulina in it—very, very good. Nature's Plus makes very good vitamins, too. Rich Life, Mega-Foods, TwinLab, Gary Null—all these are good vitamins.

In general, more expensive vitamins are better quality, but for optimum effect, read the labels. To give you some idea, a bottle of one hundred tablets of good vitamin C should cost between $10 and $15. You can get a very good calcium—120 tablets—for about $8. A customer told me she went to a laboratory to see if the Solgar calcium she had taken was absorbed into her bloodstream. The blood test showed it was absorbed quickly and was very effective. She had previously tested a generic chemical brand, and it was hardly absorbed at all. Another woman came in and bought 1000 mgs of Solgar vitamin C and took it to Pfizer Labs. She asked them to confirm how much C it actually contained. The pill tested for 1047 milligrams of C—even higher than the content description on the Solgar label.

You have to know what you're doing when you take vitamins—research very carefully. Vitamin A, vitamin D, and vitamin E are formulated in international units (IU), and they can be toxic if you overdose. Used in recommended dosages,[14] however, they are very effective.

I always tell people, "Don't be afraid. Follow the label." If you take herbs, use them for five days and rest for two days. Let your body work on its own for a few days. You have to learn how to adjust vitamins to your body. When I'm busy I need more help than when I'm relaxed.

A couple of other things: Obviously, women shouldn't smoke. But if they do, they need plenty of antioxidants and massive amounts of vitamin C. My husband is a smoker and can't stop. He takes eight beta-carotenes a day and 16,000 mg of vitamin C.

And I want to mention dong quai. It's a very important herb for women. It helps tremendously with hot flashes and levels women off. It has the same effect as ginseng—it energizes you and makes you feel very, very good. Black cohosh, too, is used to relieve menopausal symptoms and works very well.

Connie's Program

Morning:

1 Shaklee multivitamin Vital-E

Shaklee soybean Protein Performance Drink, combined with a banana and 3 big strawberries

(Connie gets all her protein in the morning because as a runner she wants it available to her muscles when she runs in the evening.)

1 Siberian ginseng capsule

800 IU vitamin E with selenium (E is important for dispersing estrogen through your bloodstream; it helps with leg cramps by keeping your blood from oxidizing.)

1 Solgar Maxi EPA capsule (Essential fatty acids keep arteries supple, clean out bad fat, and maintain good lipids—essential through menopause.)

3 triple-strength lecithin (1380 mg per capsule)

6 Shaklee alfalfa tablets (Rich in minerals, deodorizes the body, aids digestion—very good for bones.)

1 1000 mg vitamin C with magnesium and 50 mg zinc

Afternoon:

1 Shaklee Multi-Vitamin Vital-E

1 capsule combined royal jelly/bee pollen

3 triple-strength lecithin (1380 mg a capsule)

1 Solgar Maxi EPA capsule

Evening:

6 Shaklee alfalfa tablets

1 Siberian ginseng capsule

10,000 IU vitamin E oil for the inside of the vagina, along with K-Y jelly every day for extra lubrication

1 bottle of TwinLab Hydra Fuel—a potassium

carbohydrate drink to prevent leg cramps and give Connie long-term energy before her nightly run

Diet

Primarily vegetarian diet—minimal amounts of fish and chicken, lots of fruits and vegetables, brown rice, lentil or pea soup at least twice a week. She drinks 10 glasses of water a day.

Exercise

Exercises daily—runs 3 miles during the week, and on the weekends she runs 5 miles and bikes fifteen miles.

Lilli

Homeopathy, Chiropractic, and Ch'i Kong

Lilli is a pretty, petite forty-five-year-old brunette who looks twenty-five, and although she says looking young is in her genes, she seriously works at balancing her body and improving her health. She is married and works as a freelance photographer.

Lilli has been actively involved with many different alternate therapies for over fifteen years. Her exploration into natural treatments and mind/body therapies have been rewarding, but she has no problem with conventional medicine. Lilli sees a gynecologist regularly, although her general practitioner is a homeopath. She says, "I'd like women to understand that being in good health is a long-term commitment. You have to learn to pay attention and take control of your own health and your own body."

Lilli went into menopause when she was forty-one years old. She recounts:

At first I didn't have any symptoms, except my periods were messed up and when they came, there was a lot of pain. I lost my dad that year, so I thought that this had to be stress-related and was sure it would calm down. But instead I began getting severe hot flashes all day long, all up and down my body. I felt I wanted to rip my skin off. It was horrible. This sensation would come up my spine, my heart would palpitate, I'd get this racing feeling in my body. I couldn't concentrate, I couldn't sleep.

Because of my age, my gynecologist prescribed the drug Bellergal (for symptomatic relief of menopausal symptoms) instead of estrogen, but it didn't work. So the doctor recommended I take estrogen just for the summer—heat exacerbates hot flashes—to see what would happen. Within six weeks, I was worse. I hated the way my body smelled on estrogen. And instead of increasing energy, it zapped it. Things that were supposed to happen, didn't.

I went to my naturopathic doctor, and nothing he gave me worked, either.

Evening primrose oil didn't work. Upping my vitamin E didn't work. Different herb formulas—none of them worked to relieve the hot flashes. Finally, I found this chiropractor-kinesiologist who knew exactly what was going on. It was the beginning of getting my body together.

He told me that menopause had drained my adrenals, and that was starting to affect my immune system, which was why I was getting sick all the time. He tested the vitamins by placing each one on my body. Chiropractors use various techniques to test substances on your body. Kinesiology, like acupuncture, uses the concept of meridians to do the testing. A substance like an herb or vitamin is placed on the center meridians between your breasts; some kinesiologists prefer testing under the tongue. A leg or arm muscle goes physically weak or reacts strongly when the body can't accept a substance. But the muscle resistance remains strong when a substance works for you.

After testing, he said nothing I had been taking was working. The doctor threw out my whole bag of vitamins, and we started all over and found new supplements that would help me. For example, I was on 800 IU of vitamin E. He took me down to 200 IU because the quality of this supplement was so much superior to my original E, it was all my body needed. Once I was on a program, he kept monitoring me, eliminating some things and adding others, until my body was functioning normally. The idea is to get your body to kick in, to do its own job. I used to think more was better and you just keep taking vitamins. It isn't so.

I worked with him for a year and a half and felt a million times better, but not a hundred percent. I learned about other forms of kinesiology that work deeper at the cell level and found a practitioner I consult regularly now. He uses kinesiology in conjunction with homeopathy, flower essences, and nutrition. He works with what are called "core level" substances to treat structural, emotional, and physiological problems.

Along with the hormonal problems, I began to develop some neurological symptoms and consulted my medical doctor, who had incorporated homeopathy into my practice.

I asked her if she thought the hormonal and neurological problems were connected. I was so relieved when she said, "Absolutely!" She explained that menopause demands many tasks from the different body systems, and most doctors are unaware of the demands. Both my homeopathic doctor and my kinesiologist knew what I was doing. Although they didn't consult with each other, they each agreed, through me, that it was working. I was taking certain vitamins and herbs from him and homeopathic remedies from her. Professionals who work in this area are very open to collaboration.

I now regulate myself. I go off homeopathy when I feel it's not necessary and put myself back on the program when I feel I need the support. After a while, you intuitively know what your body needs. It's been my personal experience that you can put a program together for yourself without help during the years you're healthy, but once you start having real problems, you really need to check in with someone who can monitor your progress.

Another important part of my program is Ch'i Kong. Ch'i kong is a Chinese deep breathing exercise that teaches you to tap into ch'i, the vital energy force in your body. Internal ch'i is believed to help prevent disease and can help the body heal itself. External ch'i affects other people. Ch'i kong masters are said to be able to project their energy and, without touch, perform remarkable tasks like moving inanimate objects across a room or curing illness.

I was first introduced to ch'i kong through a massage therapist who told me that ch'i kong had helped get her through certain emotional states by allowing the energy of those states to pass through her.

I was immediately intrigued, I started exploring and went to see a man who does contact ch'i kong—different from the personal exercises. I had four sessions with him. During the first two he physically works on your body, and in the second two sessions you stand in front of him in a dark room, and inexplicably you just start to move. My body began to move to the rhythm of his energy. No one tells you anything. Your body just starts following the energy. It was wild. I had never done anything like this. After those sessions, I was in another state for days.

I also learned a more accessible form of ch'i kong I can do myself—a standing meditation that teaches you not only to use your own energy, but how to tap into "universal" energy—the energy outside yourself.

I am learning to be conscious of the presence of the energy all the time so I can draw on that strength when I need it. You have to get to a certain calmness in your body to be aware of it. It's strange. I realize that the longer I study ch'i kong, the more my ability increases since it centers your emotional state, your physical state, even the way your body will accept the various substances you're taking. Since I started practicing ch'i kong every day, my digestion is better. Ch'i kong works on the body at the cell level, too—just like homeopathy—it works in the basic biochemical way our bodies operate.

I also use different kinds of massage. I used to have it frequently, but I need it less now that I am more in charge of my own ship. It's very valuable. One type of deep muscle massage I use is called neuromuscular integration (SOMA). Not as intense as Rolfing, it works on the same principle—your muscles hold memories and emotions, and working those areas releases them.

I also use another masseuse for a pure physical hands-on. She just gets in and takes apart all the muscles.

Lilli's Maintenance Program

Daily:

Calcium—1200 mg

Vitamin C—2000 mg plus bioflavonoids

SOD (superoxide dismutase—a body oxygenator that helps fight off infections)

Once every other month:

10 pellets sepia (a homeopathic remedy "that seems to be formulated for my personal health and well-being")

Interchange with 10 pellets lachesis and sulphur (two other homeopathic remedies)

Diet

A healthy diet: 70 percent vegetarian/30 percent other

Lots of greens: broccoli, spinach, Swiss chard; a salad every day, especially the dark green salads like arugula and watercress

Lots of cooked vegetables; very little dairy

Exercise

Bicycle (3 times a week, 20 minutes) for cardiovascular support

Ch'i kong daily

Nancy

Vitamins and Minerals

Nancy, at eighty-eight, still lives alone and enjoys great health. She looks fit, has real energy and vitality, cooks all her own meals, gardens, and takes care of her house. Interested in everything, she is strongly involved in staying healthy, taking care of her body, and taking vitamins.

Before beginning her vitamin regimen, Nancy had a complicated medical history. At thirty-eight she had an early hysterectomy, and her uterus and one ovary were removed. That surgery was followed two years later by a lumpectomy for an encapsulated malignant breast tumor. At the time, the only postsurgical treatment recommended was preventive—X rays every year for five years. When Nancy was fifty she began to have terrible back pains and seizures that made it all but impossible to move, as well as night sweats, hot flashes, and vaginal dryness. Her menopausal symptoms were the least of her concerns, and she says, "I just couldn't think about them."

Her X rays showed evidence of osteoporosis—the cause of the pain—and the doctor's advice was, "Take codeine three times a day, and go to bed." But her husband was troubled by the prospect of long-term codeine use and began researching alternatives. Adele Davis—one of the early advocates of vitamins and diet—had recently published a book, and after reading it, her husband spoke with the owner of a local health food store—an expert on vitamins—for his advice. Armed with his suggestions, "my husband wrote to Adele Davis for her approval of the regimen, and then he put me on it."

Little by little, after several months of following the program, the back seizures stopped. Nancy began to feel better and told her brother, who is a doctor, about what she was doing for her osteoporosis. He said, "They don't know much about osteoporosis, but eventually you're going to be bent over and you'll probably be in a wheelchair." Nancy told him, "I will *never* be in a wheelchair, and I'll never be bent." She still had some pain, but over time even that lessened, and by about 1960 she was doing work around the house, gardening, walking, and swimming. If her back tired, she'd sit on a straight chair with a pillow behind her.

Nancy also says that the hot flashes, night sweats, and vaginal dryness disappeared with the back pain.

Nancy's husband also began his own vitamin regimen when she started hers. In 1989, at ninety-one years old and after fifty-eight years of marriage in what Nancy describes as a "very, very close" relationship, he passed away. In 1993 Nancy was still on the same program, doing everything she wants to do, and she stands straight and tall. Asked how she feels about growing older, she says, "I've been on this vitamin and mineral regimen for over thirty years. I may be eighty-eight now, but I never think of myself as elderly because I don't feel old.

"Helen Hayes passed away not so long ago. I saw all of her plays, and I remember something she said in a review of her life: 'Be active. No matter how old you are, you've got to be active; otherwise, you rust.' "

Nancy's Aging Gracefully Program

I begin every morning with 30 mg of coenzyme Q-10, manufactured by Bioenergy Nutrients. [Coenzyme Q-10 is an antioxidant that greatly enhances the immune system, benefits mental functioning, and slows down the aging process.] At lunchtime I take 100 mg of vitamin B_6 and 500 mg of chelated magnesium. [B_6 affects the quality of one's physical and mental health, promoting red blood cell formation. Necessary for the nervous system and normal brain functioning, it helps strengthens immune system functioning. Magnesium is an essential mineral that enhances enzyme activity and can help prevent depression and muscle weakness. Chelation is a process that attaches the mineral to a protein molecule to help the body absorb it more easily.]

I take 1000 mg of rosehips vitamin C, also at lunchtime, along with an additional B_{12} dot (500 mcg) that I place under my tongue. Also on my regimen are 50 mg of natural chelated manganese gluconate and 50 mg of natural amino acid chelated zinc. Manganese works with the B complex I take and generally makes me feel better. Zinc is good for the immune system.

I used to take a B-50 complex vitamin, but three years ago I had to sell the house and felt very stressed, so I went to my vitamin consultant and we upped my B-50 complex to B-100. Containing all the B vitamins, it really helped, and I take that at lunch, too.

One of the alternative doctors I listen to on the radio suggested taking 500 mg of silica for my hair, nails, and bones, so I take that. I get so much information from these radio shows.

At dinner, I take 400 IU of vitamin E and another 1000 mg vitamin C rosehips. The vitamins I take, by the way are manufactured by Price, Inc.

The food I grew up on was very simple. My family's Italian—I was born in Sicily, south of Palermo, but we moved to Brooklyn when I was seven. When my mother cooked she used good wholesome food, lots of fresh vegetables and fresh fruits. In those days we ate everything in season. We were not big meat eaters. Mostly we ate a nice plate of pasta with vegetables like cauliflower, broccoli, and peas. We ate beans. When we had meat, it was just a small piece. And of course we ate fish. The man used to come every day in a cart with a wooden icebox loaded with fresh fish.

We seldom had sweets—only on holidays or if you went to a wedding or christening.

We drank cream soda, sarsaparilla, and seltzer. Sometimes we would mix sarsaparilla with cream soda. And of course I always drank a lot of water. My father used to make wine, and on holidays we would mix the wine with seltzer.

The food I eat now is still very simple—like the gourmet cooking of today—and I learned how to prepare much of it from my mother.

At breakfast I have cereal. Usually I buy the Health Valley brand—amaranth, oat bran, kashi. I eat it with fruit I cooked myself: prunes or apricots or a handful of raisins and a thin slice of orange peel and a thin slice of lemon peel. I never use sugar. I let the fruit soak for a while, then start cooking it over a low flame for about a half hour. When it cools off I put this mix in jars and refrigerate it. I usually put it over my cereal in the morning. Sometimes I have cooked cereal—this morning I had Wheatena—and I eat that with molasses.

For lunch I usually make tuna-fish salad with lots of onion, grated carrots, and celery. I mix a little mayonnaise with yogurt and add a little lemon juice and some ripe black olives. I then make a sandwich with it on no-salt, whole-wheat bread. I serve it with hearts of escarole, and then I have an apple and my vitamins.

Other times I make escarole and beans for lunch. I cook the greens. Then, in a separate pan, I sauté garlic in olive oil. When the greens are cooked, I add them to the garlic. I drain a can of beans and put them in the pan and let it all simmer. That's it, and let me tell you, it's delicious.

For dinner, I seldom eat meat. What I do instead is buy veal bones, when they have them, with lots of meat on them. I put them under the broiler and brown them, then put them in a pot with water. I use lots of onion, minced garlic, tomatoes, leeks, parsley, and carrots. I add dill and sometimes use barley or brown rice. I finish by tying some peppercorns, a bay leaf, and a few cloves in cheesecloth and flick it into the pot and then let it all cook.

I exercise regularly by walking and gardening, and I still do all my own housework. Maybe that's why

I don't have osteoporosis. I stand straight, and I'm strong enough to do everything I want to do. Taking good care of myself isn't hard; after all, I've been doing it the whole second half of my life, almost forty years now. But I keep learning new things about staying healthy all the time.

Neila

Tibetan Herbs, Vitamins, Fem 50

Neila is a fifty-year-old psychotherapist whose gynecologist has been tracking her health for several years because of erratic positive Pap smears. The pathology reports could only confirm that cell changes had occurred, but they could not determine if the condition was dangerous. Her gynecologist told her positive Paps were a common side effect of menopause, but as a precaution the doctor recommended a cervical biopsy in an office procedure. This "allows the pathologist to examine the full thickness of the cervical epithelium rather than just the surface layer of cells obtained from a Pap smear."[15]

Knowing her body was undergoing a change, Neila decided to consult Dr. Yeshi Donden—physician to the Dalai Llama—who was in New York for an annual two-week visit to exchange information on ways of practicing medicine with Western doctors. Tibetan medicine, based on the medical teachings of Buddha, is concentrated in four texts called the Four Tantras. Treatments are basically herbal, but accessory therapies such as acupuncture or surgery may be used if herbs do not provide a cure. She says:

Dr. Donden diagnosed me by taking my pulse, checking my urine, and observing my body. Speaking through a translator, he told me I was healthy and confirmed that my body was going through a change. I was given some Tibetan herbs to deal specifically with the changes going on in my cervix and ovaries, but I don't know what they are. I take them on the basis of my faith in him. My last Pap smear was negative, but it's difficult to know whether it was the herbs or the biopsy.

A group of friends, all in different stages of menopause, came together at our house, and we exchanged our own experiences as a way of finding out more about menopause. We really learned from each other. I've also been doing a lot of reading on the subject. I'm not convinced that taking synthetic estrogen into my body is worth the long-term risk, so I'm wide open to dealing naturally with my hot flashes and any other symptoms that may develop. But at this stage, with my own intelligence as a guide, I've put a program together for myself, and it seems to be working.

Neila's Entering Menopause Program

Daily:

Dr. Donden's Tibetan herbs
1 multivitamin capsule
1 C complex capsule
1 vitamin E capsule (400 mg)

1 calcium/magnesium tablet (1200 mg)
1 raw adrenal capsule (for increasing energy)
1 Fem 50 (for hot flashes)

Fem 50 is an over-the-counter vitamin/mineral/food supplement recommended by a woman I've known for years. Fem 50 has made a real difference in my life. Last Christmas I stopped using it, and the hot flashes came back. As soon as I started taking it again, the hot flashes stopped, so I know it works. The ingredients in Fem 50, according to the label, are 50 mg black cohosh, 50 IU vitamin E, 50 mg vitamin B_6, 50 mg pantothenic acid, 50 mg vitamin C, 50 mg calcium, 225 mcg iodine, 150 mg wild yam root, 100 mg licorice root, 100 mg false unicorn root, 100 mg dong quai, 50 mg passion flower, and 50 mg PABA.

Except for the iodine, all the other ingredients in Fem 50 are vitamin or mineral supplements or common herbs for menopause (see page 197).

Diet

Vegetables, fruits, grains, some chicken and fish, and very little meat.

Exercise

Yoga, usually twice a week.
Walking 2 miles every other day.

Susan

Vitamins, Minerals, Herbs, and Exercise

A fifty-one-year-old writer and editor, Susan specializes in the fields of graphic design and women's health. When she went into menopause six years ago, the knowledge gained from years of activism in the women's health field became personal. Doing research is a writer's task, but taking charge of one's own body is a basic tenet of feminism, and Susan set about learning what was happening to hers. She was unwilling to take estrogen since her mother has had two mastectomies, which meant Susan was genetically predisposed to cancer. Alternative medicine was a necessity for her. Susan tells her story:

I have always had rough periods, I have always had PMS, I have always had cramps. Menopause meant very erratic periods for a couple of years followed by fewer periods and PMS that lasted for weeks. In the beginning I tried to help myself physically. I took ginseng and I took evening primrose oil. I did lots of exercise and drank no alcohol, ate no chocolate, and used no salt—I was very good because I didn't want to feel like a maniac. But my PMS was still a problem. I consulted a medical doctor who used vitamin therapy, but he overmedicated my thyroid, so I stopped seeing him. I went to a chiropractor who treated my symptoms with homeopathic remedies, but my PMS persisted for nine weeks, followed a few weeks after that by another bout that lasted eleven weeks. The chiropractor recommended I see a specialist who used a broader range of treatments for menopausal symptoms.

The therapist I consulted had a multitherapeutic approach to health problems, and she put me on all kinds of Chinese herbs as well as homeopathic remedies, and she also did massage and performed acupuncture. It took a year and a half of once-a-month visits before I was PMS asymptomatic.

I think alternative medicine is very hard to do on your own because you need the right herbs in the right dosages. I don't know, frankly, what herbs I'm taking, but I don't feel I need to know. I trust my therapist when she gives me herbs. I trust her when she puts in an acupuncture needle. I trust my chiropractor when he manipulates my hipbone. And what's essential is this trust. But to work this way I think you need to have a certain kind of mind-set and sensibility. It requires taking control over what happens to your body.

I have a friend who suddenly stopped having her period and went through hideous depressions. I can suggest all I want to, but she would never consider doing what I'm doing. It takes a willingness to experiment and a real dissatisfaction with conventional treatment. I personally don't trust Western medicine. But that doesn't mean I don't use medical doctors when I need them. I think a balance is necessary. I believe you have to have both, because conventional medicine can sometimes do things alternative medicine can't do. As an example, while I was under alternative care, I had my thyroid tested by a different medical doctor. According to the conventional diagnosis, my thyroid was low and I would probably need to stay on medication for the rest of my life. I decided to take the prescribed drug but also work with my alternative therapist on this condition.

It took three years to accomplish, but my thyroid functions normally, now—primarily because of alternative medicine. And my medical doctor took me off medication because the lab tests showed I didn't need it anymore. I think that is pretty significant.

In 1991 I went through a fairly profound depression despite working with her healer.

I just started feeling like I made terrible mistakes in my life. I began questioning everything! I'm single. I'm alone, and oh, my God, how am I going to cope—I mean, it was awful. Classic menopausal. So I decided to take a workshop through a midlife counseling service. I took it twice, and it triggered me into wanting to explore menopause more. While attending the workshop, I was reading a book called *Transformation Through Menopause.*[16] It is very much an exploration of body, mind, and spirit and how they all work together at menopause. It explains that what we go through is natural and that there's nothing clinically wrong with us. Then suddenly—and I can't explain how or why—I was no longer depressed. I thought, I made the right decisions. I'm okay. I can live with myself.

The most important thing a woman can do is listen to her body and try to give it what it needs. Don't get scared, and try not to become overwhelmed by all the change—on every level. Instead of going into denial and saying "It's not happening to me," try to find ways to cope. Allow yourself time and space to solve the problems, and don't think it's going to be easy, quick, take a pill, it's over. Forget that. Remember there's a reason why your body is going through this.

I ignored my body for years. I took it for granted. I have used this time as a way of getting in touch with parts of myself that I never have related to before. Menopause has turned into a very valuable and rich experience for me.

Susan's Midage Health Regimen

Daily

2000 mg vitamin C (Susan uses a chewable form or crystals dissolved in water for better absorption.)
A multivitamin high in B vitamins
Natural chelated calcium/magnesium (500 mg calcium, 250 mg magnesium)
800 IU vitamin E
Vitamin E oil applied internally for vaginal dryness as needed
Royal jelly to help support the immune system
500 mg ginseng
Spirulina

Susan began taking spirulina after she had a reaction to an injection of Demerol she was given for oral surgery. She says, "I couldn't keep a thought in my brain for more than thirty seconds; it was awful." Her chiropractor suggested using spirulina as a way of cleansing the brain cells.

Diet

Primarily vegetarian

Rice, whole grains, beans, tofu, lots of vegetables, but I will occasionally have meat. I went to a church supper with relatives, and they served ham. So I ate ham. I eat tuna fish occasionally or have chicken when I go out. I was raised in a meat-and-potatoes family, and I thought I would fall apart and have no energy if I became a vegetarian. That was a total misconception. I also drink eight glasses of water a day.

Exercise

3–4 times a week:
20 minutes on the treadmill
Swim ½ mile
100 curls and weight lifting on the weight machines

Deborah

Commercial Vitamin Compound

Deborah is a high-powered real estate broker in New York City. She looks much younger than her fifty years and has always enjoyed good health and great energy. She sails and golfs and is very athletic. So, at age forty-nine, when she started having terrible night sweats accompanied by anxiety and fear, making sleep impossible, she never connected it to menopause, and neither did her doctors. Her puzzled family physician thought she might have a brain tumor and ordered a scan. Her brain was quite intact. And, as she says, she finally used her brain to begin doing her own research. It didn't take long for her to realize she was in menopause. Because Deborah comes from a medical family, she was reluctant to take estrogen since she was convinced drugs always had side effects. Her symptoms were becoming intolerable to her when a friend suggested a vitamin regimen developed by an Idaho manufacturer. Even though Deborah was skeptical, her friend suggested she had nothing to lose. This compound is one of a line of mail-order products formulated with a Melaleuca alternifolia leaf base. After using the product for only a couple of days, her symptoms began to subside, and within a week they disappeared completely. Her energy came back, and she has had a general feeling of well-being ever since.

Deborah's Treatment for All Menopausal Symptoms

Twice a day:

1 Mel-Vita capsule—consisting of 19 essential vitamins and minerals

1 Mela-Cal capsule—a combination of magnesium and phosphorus in "exclusive copyrighted proportions with vitamin C and D."

The accompanying literature describes the products this way: "Melaleuca's patented fructose compounding bonds minerals to small, easily absorbed fructose molecules, which are readily recognized and assimilated by the body's cells. The unique 'delivery' system is designed to ensure that the minerals and vital nutrients are not merely flushed through the body without effect." For more information, write to Melaleuca, Inc., Idaho Falls, Idaho, 83402.

Margaret

Herbs, Cell Salts, and Nutrition

Margaret is fifty-four years old and divorced, the editor of an international graphics magazine. She entered a convent when she was eighteen years old, leaving at age twenty-five before her final vows. She feels that those seven years ultimately shaped her attitude toward her body until menopause, when everything changed. She says:

Growing up, I never understood the girls who could talk about menstruation as a normal cycle of life, and the fact that they could swim or play games anytime they wanted was inexplicable. For me, it was *Wuthering Heights* every time—tremendously melodramatic, always painful, and physically debilitating. But even if I were in pain or had cramps, I got up, put on my habit, dragged myself to chapel. The body was nothing to give in to even if you fainted. The body's role was to carry your soul around. Catholic girls have a hard time anyway in terms of relating to their bodies, but in my case, the fact that my periods were always painful made it difficult to ignore my body.

I discovered later that the reason my periods were so

erratic and why I had so much pain was that one of my ovaries was overdeveloped and the other one was nonfunctional. I did not look forward to menopause.

For two years I managed to get hot flashes during each menstrual cycle, so everything kept going—my aching pain, the cramps, and also hot flashes at night so severe that my bed was soaked. (I think everyone going through menopause needs to have a good supply of 100 percent cotton sheets. Synthetic fibers exacerbate hot flashes.) Then my periods stopped, but I still had these other symptoms. I ended up in an emergency room after I fainted. My body was totally out of kilter, and no one could tell me it was just menopause.

I was put on the lowest dosage of estrogen, but within a week my skin started getting very tight and my body started screaming. It was horrific. I felt as if I were blowing up from inside and becoming a taut plastic bag. It was worse than the hot flashes.

My doctor had no other suggestions for me, so I began asking my friends what I could do. I was introduced to a naturopath, who put me on a program not only to relieve the menopausal symptoms, but also to balance my body.

Once I started on this program of natural treatments, I could see and feel past the physical. I'd say it took menopause for me to just accept myself. Finally I can embrace being my age. I think this is the best time of my life. There is no more constant pain, no more hot flashes to incinerate me, no more gaining ten pounds every month from water retention. But the release from these brutal cycles is pretty dramatic, too. It's wrong to use the word *comfortable* in trying to explain how I am now. But I inhabit myself more than I have before.

My sexual attitudes have also changed. Before, whenever there was an emotional trigger, I felt very vulnerable, in a defensive position. If a man becomes aware of me as a woman now, it's not unnerving. I can accept that I'm sexual, sexually active, and may actually be sexually attractive to a man. I can say "no" or I can say "yes." But I am no longer being held hostage by my body. I did what my body told me to do, bypassing my brain, my emotions. While I was going through all my hormonal dilemmas, someone pointed out to me that "the sexiest organ in your body is your brain." I remembered that when I was watching television in Europe and I saw real women on the tube with real lines on their faces that they had earned—*and* brains. That's what makes people glow in the dark, sexually, emotionally, and in every way. It has nothing to do with the body or hormones at any age.

Growing older? I'd say glory in it. Don't look in the mirror and compare yourself with anyone. See what's really in the mirror. A friend of mine explained the beautiful woman routine to me. It's remarkably effective, not only for this time, but any time. Basically, you see yourself as a very beautiful woman and walk around like one, rehearsing the parts of yourself that reach out to the world, and you will see that the responses to you are not about age, but about how you see yourself.

There is a Doris Lessing novel, *Summer Before the Dark,* in which a woman in her fifties is hiding out from her family in London. She rents a little basement flat to give herself some time of her own. There is a building site close by where men are working, and the first time she walks out there are screams, yells, catcalls, and whistles. Aware that she is the object of all this excitement, she deliberately wears a head scarf the next time she comes out and walks kind of hunched over and acts terribly preoccupied. She is totally ignored by them. It's what we put out that gets the response back.

I want the rest of my life to be glamorous. I was always afraid of being attractive and sexual and glamorous. It was too much then. But now I can be all of those things.

Margaret's Program

This program is divided into three parts: menopausal symptoms, counteracting the effects of smoking, and body balancing.

Menopausal Symptoms

Morning:
1 black cohosh

To treat hot flashes, night sweats, and vaginal dryness, I was put on black cohosh. It's an herb with estrogenic qualities. My naturopath started me out with two capsules a day, but I only need one capsule now to feel fine.

Black cohosh is mild, so my naturopath thought we could encourage my adrenals to pump out a bit more estrogen with the following supplementation:

Morning and evening:
1 capsule raw adrenal
1 capsule raw thymus

Counteracting the Effects of Smoking

Morning and evening:

1 capsule nettle

1 capsule mullein

Inhale steam from boiling ½ cup apple cider diluted with water to clear morning mucous out of the lungs.

Body Balancing

Cell salts are tiny homeopathic pills, the basis for improving overall health.

3 pills twice a day of the following:

#2 Calc. Phos. cell salts to help digestion and build red blood cells

#3 Calc. Sulph. cell salts as a blood purifier

#4 Ferr. Phos. cell salts to deal with lung congestion from smoking

#7 Kali. Sulph. cell salts to take care of bronchial problems due to smoking

#10 Nat. Phos. cell salts to aid digestion (see page 218 for individual cell salt descriptions)

Morning and evening:

500 mg B_{12} capsule to improve digestion

3 times a day, for digestion:

5 kelp pills

5 garlic pills

Diet

I decided I needed to lose weight—it's been an on-and-off struggle for most of my life—but once I started my herb and vitamin routine, I thought losing weight was incidental to learning how to eat the right way to stay healthy. I talked to my thin, healthy friends, and they gave me this advice: If you eat lots of vegetables, fruits, grains, and legumes, and you don't eat fats and sugar and junk food, it won't be long before you crave the "good" food. I'm not sure about craving vegetables, but not eating excessive proteins and carbohydrates and eating at regular times has helped me lose weight, and I plan to keep it off.

Because I always have digestion problems, I begin every day with a cup of homemade vegetable stock with one tablespoon each of raw bran and raw flax seed. (Gently heat and swallow without chewing for roughage.)

Generally, this is what I eat:

2 ounces of "good fat"—olive oil
2 to 4 ounces of protein every day (tofu, fish, organic chicken, and so forth)
At least 4 helpings of vegetables every day
3 portions of grains: pasta, bread, rice, and so on
2 or 3 pieces of fruit
8 glasses of water a day

In general, I try to avoid anything that doesn't have a natural sugar base, like fructose. But I have a piece of killer chocolate cake in my refrigerator just in case, although I'm ready to throw it away because it doesn't appeal to me anymore. Now I find I don't overeat madly one day and eat nothing the next.

I feel a lot more alive now that I'm on a program

I control. I had no idea how desensitized I was to just about everything until I started paying attention to my body. I still smoke and drink, but now I know how many calories go with every glass of wine, and I'm consciously choosing my substitutes.

Exercise

Stretching exercises and walking every day
½ hour on the stationary bike twice a week

Meditation

Every day for stress

I am actually amazed that I am following this routine—nonbeliever that I am—but I just do it by rote now. I feel better, and I don't want to take the chance that I'll feel so unstable again.

I take a hot apple cider vinegar bath at night to help me to sleep. I used to be exhausted in the morning, but the bath revs up my system and clears my bloodstream, and I wake up differently. It's a genuine kind of rest.

I don't feel anything like fifty-four going on fifty-five. I have a different kind of energy from different places now that I do basic things to help myself.

Marcia

Homeopathic Remedies

In 1985, Marcia, a forty-four-year-old woman whose complicated menstrual history included extreme PMS and severe reactions to pregnancies followed by miscarriages, braced herself for a difficult menopause. Soon after her periods became erratic, she began to experience the full range of menopausal symptoms. The hot flashes were particularly intense. Marcia says:

I would get dressed three times before I left the house to go to work. I'd take a shower, and while I dried my hair, I would become soaking wet and have to sit down and blow my hair again. My gynecologist told me I had a hormone imbalance but that I was not in menopause. When he put me on low-dose hormone replacement therapy (.3 mg), the symptoms disappeared immediately and my periods were regular again. But before long I began gaining weight. I was eating when I wasn't even hungry. My blood pressure was up, and the flashes began coming back. My doctor doubled my hormone dose, but almost immediately I began getting headaches that escalated into migraines every day. I even blacked out at work. I complained to my doctor, and he said, "It's not from the hormones."

But when my neurologist scheduled me for a CAT scan, I called my gynecologist and pressed him about the hormones. I reminded him that my mother had had ovarian cancer. He checked my chart and said, "Well, I see here that you also have a history of strokes in your family, so I'm taking you off hormones."

Once off the hormones, the headaches stopped, but the hot flashes, the night sweats, and the mood swings started again. My gynecologist said it was an allergic reaction to the synthetic hormones I had been taking and recommended 1200 mg of vitamin E a day. I upped it, I lowered it, but it didn't help at all.

A chiropractor I was seeing about a back problem suggested taking a homeopathic combination pill called Feminine* for hot flashes. He told me to put one under my tongue. I didn't expect it to work right away. Nothing can do that, I thought. Well, it was amazing. I stood in ninety-degree heat in the sun with this pill under my tongue and I didn't perspire—not even a sweat bead on my upper lip.

With that, I began an intense exploration into alternative therapies. Even though the hot flashes were much better, I still had them, and the compound didn't help enough with my other symptoms—weight gain, headaches, depression, and so forth. But I now knew that something besides estrogen could help relieve hot flashes and that maybe there were alternatives for the other symptoms as well. I started reading and researching, which I had never done. My friends clipped

*Available through Biological Homeopathic Industries, Inc.: 11600 Cochiti, S.E., Albuquerque, New Mexico 87123.

magazine articles and sent them to me. Then one day I was talking with the owner of a pharmacy that specializes in homeopathic remedies, and he gave me the name of a homeopathic medical doctor.

I began treatment two years ago. On the first visit I spent three hours with the doctor. She took a complete history and then gave me a combination of remedies for hot flashes, mood swings, night sweats, and general health. I really believed it would help me. I'm very skeptical about a lot of things, but I walked out quite hopeful.

I was slow to realize the changes were happening, but my close friends and my husband began to notice. Within a month I realized that I was sleeping, the mood swings weren't that bad, and I wasn't nervous. I couldn't believe the improvement.

I've now been on homeopathic remedies for two years, and the prescriptions are constantly being readjusted. I no longer need anything to control my nervous stomach because I don't have one. Insomnia is still one of my biggest problems, but that too is beginning to improve. I now believe that I've had a hormone imbalance my whole life. Most doctors never ask you any questions. When I was growing up no one really cared when I complained about feeling sick. But I remember having a very low tolerance for drugs.

Marcia's Homeopathic Program

The homeopathic prescriptions given to Marcia are different from those written by medical doctors. For example, her most recent prescription contains ten separate remedies in different doses to be taken at different times of the day as well as different days of the week. The three nighttime remedies are to be taken one hour before bedtime; formulated specifically for Marcia's combination of symptoms and physical problems, they would have very little general use for menopause.

However, in examining Marcia's prescriptions over the two-year period she has been treated with homeopathy, I noticed that several common homeopathic remedies—often mentioned by herbalists and homeopaths in connection with menopause—are included. (See Dr. Elmaleh, page 50.)

Sepia is prescribed for the emotional stress that causes exhaustion and chronic constipation. Marcia's dosage is 18 c.

Lachesis is for hot flashes that are particularly difficult in the morning. Marcia takes 9 c, 3 pellets every morning.

Pulsatilla alleviates hot flashes around the face. Marcia's dosage: 9 c, 3 pellets, M-W-F.

Ignatia is for hot flashes and constipation. Marcia takes 9 c, 3 pellets every morning.

Belladonna relieves headaches. Marcia takes 5 c every hour until she gets relief.

Sulfuricum acidium, to be used when hot flashes are extreme. Marcia's dosage: 5 c, twice a day.

What is most important about homeopathy is its specificity with regard to a symptom. Hot flashes combined with sleeplessness calls for one kind of remedy, while another might treat flushes of the face. A remedy like kreosotum is used when a woman complains of burning heat all over the body. If you are under the care of a homeopath and the nature of a hot flash changes, the remedy may also need to be changed. Or you may be taking several different remedies for the symptoms as they occur.

It is, of course, possible to prescribe for yourself by using existing resource books to match your symptoms with the remedies. The challenge is the same if you choose to work with a homeopath, but chances are a homeopath will save you time and the remedies may be more accurate. Either way it is often a long-term process—as Marcia has discovered—but with patience it is an exploration that does cure.

Barbara

Chiropractic and Nutrition

Barbara is fifty-five years old. She is married and the mother of two grown sons. When she is not working with her husband in his architectural firm, she plays competitive amateur tennis. A bout with bronchial asthma forced her to leave New York City for eight months to rest. Adrenalin was prescribed for her breathing, but she stopped using it because it is habit-forming.

"Your whole body locks when you stop taking Adrenalin. I couldn't move my arms. I was all swollen, and the doctor kept insisting that I had to take it again. I was determined not to do that, so I found a chiropractor who would manipulate my body to get me moving. I went to him five days a week for about three weeks. I realized that without taking any medication, I was getting better. I tried to explain to my doctor that the chiropractor was only using massage to open my back and my lungs. I told him I felt so much better. The doctor, who was very competent, became extremely angry. Since I intended to keep getting chiropractic treatment, I stopped seeing him for a while."

Then Barbara went into menopause, with classic symptoms—irritability, insomnia, headaches, and hot flashes. With a family history of cancer on both sides, as well as her other physical problems, she was looking for a safe alternative to hormones. She recounts:

My father died of kidney cancer, my grandmother died from liver cancer, and my mother's family is riddled with cancer, but even then, six different doctors said, "Take estrogen, the benefits are worth the risk." The last of those doctors—a reproductive endocrinologist and strong advocate for hormone replacement—refused to continue the consultation because Barbara insisted on being offered some safe alternative for her symptoms. "I asked each of them how they could even suggest that I take estrogen once they knew my family history. They all said they couldn't help me if I wouldn't take estrogen.

A friend had been telling me for years about the things her chiropractor/nutritionist had done for her, but I never believed her, not even after a chiropractor treated my Adrenalin reaction without drugs. Finally, with no other options and because my friend was persistent, I went to see him. My menopausal symptoms were out of control, and I had a skyrocketing cholesterol level. I admit I was a real doubting Thomas, until he tested oat bran under my tongue. I had a wild reflex reaction. I simply couldn't keep my arms down by my side! The doctor said, "Don't ever eat oat bran again. Your body is deadly allergic to it." He proceeded to flush out my kidneys and spleen with massage for over an hour and a half. He told me to stay close to the house because I was going to be in the bathroom getting rid of the toxins in my system. I went back two days later, and he repeated the treatment. He put me on a nutritional support program to take care of the menopausal symptoms, bring down the cholesterol, and generally balance my body, which he said had been depleted by years of physical problems, allergies, and previous medications. And that's how I became a convert to alternative therapy.

When I was going through menopause, my regular doctor wanted me to have a hysterectomy for three grapefruit-size fibroid tumors. "Trust me," my doctor said. And with that I walked out of the office. I had no intention of having a hysterectomy. But in May, soon after my visit, I broke my leg and it had to be put into a cast. I didn't want my leg to atrophy, so I started doing leg lifts—three hundred to five hundred a day in addition to four hundred scissors, crossing your legs front and back.

During the first month I had a very bad period—hemorrhaging and blood clots. But the second month was much different, less bleeding and less clotting. By the third month I was sure my stomach was smaller and softer. With fibroids, your stomach is like a pot belly and hard. I went to the library to see if I could find out whether there was any connection between exercise and my diminishing stomach. I discovered that fibroids are muscle tissue, and if you exercise a muscle, it gets smaller. The gynecologist wanted to see me in September, so I kept the appointment, and after he examined me, he said, "What have you been doing? Your fibroids are drastically smaller. I can't even *find* one of them." In four months my fibroids had reduced to the size of grapes. The doctor was amazed. He said I was a phenomenon. I said to him, "Don't you think you might have told me I had an option to hysterectomy?" He said, "It might work for one woman out of a hundred—you're the exception to the rule." The fibroids have completely disappeared now. The leg lifts helped my vaginal dryness, too. I still do a hundred and fifty a day."

Barbara's Body Balancing Program

1 Fem Estro every day
(Fem Estro is a natural support for women in menopause. It contains vitamin E, vitamin B_5, bioflavonoids, PABA, vitamin C, raw adrenal, and ginseng. Barbara started taking 3 a day, but after 2 months she needed only 2, and after 4 months she is now on a maintenance dose of 1 a day. The menopausal symptoms are gone, including hot flashes and night sweats.)

1 Multivitamin every day
(Barbara takes Energetics, an herb, vitamin-mineral thyroid compound: 1 in the morning and 1 midafternoon, with 1 prescription thyroid pill. She has been taking 3 thyroid pills for 30 years. Because she is supplementing with Energetics, her dosage is now down to 1 prescription thyroid pill. Her endocrinologist has reported that her blood test readings are normal.)

1 Acidophilus, twice a day
(maintains bacteria in the stomach)

1 400 mg vitamin E with selenium, once a day

1 B complex capsule, once a day

1 S.A.T.—contains thistle seed, artichoke concentrate, and turmeric concentrate, once a day
(Barbara was feeling very bilious, and the S.A.T. stopped the pain.)

1 Potassium aspirate capsule—mild form of potassium

(Barbara takes it to prevent leg cramps when she plays tennis—3 or 4 times a week for extra support.)

1 Undecyn, 3 times a week
(prevents or stops yeast infections)

1 Thorn Research iron picolinate, 3 times a week
(A gentle iron supplement blend. Barbara was very anemic while going through menopause. Her blood tests showed very low readings, but she could not tolerate regular iron supplements, so her chiropractor recommended iron picolinate, which is easier on her stomach. It is available only through health professionals.)

1 Core-level raw adrenal (Nutra-West), 3 times a week

Diet

I eat fish, meat, and eggs and only eat pasta once a month as a main course. I try to eat lots of vegetables. I never eat white bread. I drink four ounces of water every hour during the day—every day—stopping about six o'clock in the evening. When I play tennis I take a half-gallon jug with me.

Until last February I was on a carbohydrate diet, eating a lot of pasta with nonmeat sauces. I found I was eating less and gaining a lot of weight. I was really frustrated. My thyroid condition used to make it difficult for me to gain or lose weight, but I was gaining weight. My chiropractor said that when some women reach menopausal age, they can't metabolize carbohydrates as easily. I've reached that plateau, but as long as I stay on a high-protein diet, I can keep my weight down easily because my body *can* metabolize protein.

Exercise

Tennis—3 times a week
Weights—3 pounds for toning (50 repetitions, military presses for the upper body)
Leg lifts—75 times each leg

Laurie

Yoga, Alexander Technique, Supplements, and Diet

A "highly aggressive" strain of breast cancer was discovered in Laurie's breast in 1988 when she was forty-six years old. Lumpectomy, radiation, and chemo followed immediately. Instant menopause was the least of the changes Laurie had to deal with. In her case, breast cancer caused her to reevaluate her life and to choose alternative and unconventional directions for dealing with her work and her health. Over the years she has consulted with many alternative practitioners and has put together a program for herself that draws from the knowledge she gained. Laurie tells us:

Breast cancer and menopause pushed me into doing things and seeing things in what was for me a radical new way. I had spent my life being nearly totally unconscious of my body, treating it the way you would a car, asking only that it start when I turn on the ignition. I put the fuel in and took it to the doctor at regular intervals but had no interest in its workings.

Menopause has actually acquainted me with my body.

I can no longer afford to take my body and its health for granted, as I was able to up to my late forties, and now I give it a great deal of thought and attention. I haven't had hot flashes, although I'm aware of changes in my metabolism, which includes a sense of my own body temperature fluctuating during the day and night. Estrogen was never an option for me, even without breast cancer. I think there's enough evidence to implicate synthetic estrogen as a cancer-producing agent.

I have been studying Iyengar yoga for several years now, and I am hooked on the way it makes me feel. Not only has it provided me with great flexibility and stamina—and helped me keep my figure—but it also offers a precise way of isolating different parts of the body and understanding the interrelationships among muscles, bones, and connective tissue. The long-term benefits become obvious as I work on special poses for increasing blood flow to disks in the spine or create space in the hip sockets, which over time would cause me to lose range of motion. These exercises counteract the compressing habits of posture and normal body use.

This form of yoga is so precise that one can focus on areas where lifelong habits have caused constriction. And damage can actually be reversed. There are photographs of an eighty-year-old woman doing extraordinary yoga positions in a book called *Awakening the Spine* by Vanda Scaravelli, published by HarperCollins. These photos should be on every woman's refrigerator as graphic illustrations of our physical possibilities. Iyengar yoga is a much better answer to concerns about osteoporosis than estrogen: it teaches you to manage physical issues from inside the body. It also has so many other benefits, with no potentially dangerous side effects. The idea is that the loss of bone mass, cartilage, and connective tissue is a result of poor habits accumulating into disability of body use over time. It is a powerful idea for me because it means disability is not a function of aging per se.

I'm also learning to change habits of a lifetime through the Alexander Technique, which is complementary to yoga. Alexander deals with habitual ways of standing, sitting, and doing the things we do daily, things that unconsciously cause constriction in our nervous systems and further wear away the natural cushions in the body over time.

I take vitamins, herbs, and other supplements because no matter how well I eat, I know that my system needs added support to continue to strengthen my immune system and keep me healthy now and as I grow older.

It sounds daunting when you read the list of what I do for my health, but it doesn't feel that way. These things have become second nature and are new health-supporting habits that I prefer to my old, unconscious habits. The payoff has been in a richer, more textured inner life and awareness and a feeling of excitement and anticipation of all that will unfold in the future.

Laurie's Build the Immune System Program

Once a day:
1 multivitamin that delivers 25,000 IU of
A/beta-carotene
Twice a day:
1000 mg vitamin C
400 mg vitamin E

3 each of
#3 Calc. Sulph. cell salts
#4 Ferr. Phos. cell salts
#7 Kali. Sulph. cell salts
#9 Nat. Mur. cell salts (sodium chloride)
#12 Silica cell salts (See page 218 for the function of each.)
1 capsule echinacea with reishi and astragalus (mushrooms shown to improve immune functioning)
1 capsule chapparal (herb that purifies the blood and protects the body against formation of tumors and cancer cells)
1 capsule yellow dock (another blood-purifying herb that balances iron deficiency; used as an effective whole body toner)
1 capsule red clover (herb used to help break up growths and tumors in combination with chapparal; a blood cleanser, body relaxant)
1 capsule myrrh (herb used to help prevent or relieve infections)

Diet

I try to eat a healthy vegetarian diet (strict, with no dairy products) lots of *only* organic vegetables, leafy green and those rich in beta-carotene—an antioxidant that protects against cancer formation—like asparagus, broccoli, carrots, kale, peaches, sweet potatoes, spinach, and yellow squash.

For the first year or two after finishing my chemotherapy, to rebuild my immune system I went on a strict macrobiotic diet, a vegetarian diet based on whole grains (particularly brown rice), legumes, vegetables, and sea vegetables, with no animal fats.

Water

Bottled when out, purified water at home
(I have a theory that the fewer toxins my body has to deal with, the more time and energy it has to function at maximum efficiency.)

Exercise and Meditation

Yoga classes 3 times a week in the morning; daily 30-minute meditation
(The form of meditation is vipassana, which is an awareness meditation. One sits in a comfortable position with eyes closed, breathing in and out and paying attention to the breath.)

Baths

3 special baths a week to clear my liver: 1 cup of apple cider vinegar in hot water (see page 126 for complete instructions)

Part Four

More on Herbs, Vitamins, and Supplements

The interviews with natural health specialists and the programs of women who manage menopause without estrogen detail approaches and treatments for symptoms. But there is a wealth of information to be found in herb books, natural medicine compilations, newsletters, and more. I include a sampling of some of this information, and if it interests you, I encourage you to do further research on your own. The use of alternative therapies at menopause can lead you to a new way of handling other health problems. Take advantage of the richness and wisdom contained in these sources as well as those listed in the bibliography.

The Most Common Herbs for Menopause

These herbs, like all herbs, originate as plants, and the various parts, usually the roots and leaves, are dried and crushed or powdered before they are used. They can be the basis of medicinal teas or applied to the body as a poultice. There are outlets for dried herbs sold in bulk that need to be prepared before use, but today most people get their herbs prepackaged in capsule, pill, or tincture (liquid) form, and these are available for sale in vitamin stores and health food shops.

Finding the right menopausal herbs for your body out of the nineteen listed below can be managed by trial and error, starting with the four most commonly recommended herbs, but professional guidance will help you make educated choices. Every herb works differently on different women. It could be the dosage, it could be the herb, it could be the combination you are taking. When you take herbs they begin to work immediately, but it takes time to see the results. Using any herb for one month will give you enough time to judge whether it is effective.

A mild dose of any of the following herbs is 1 capsule in the morning and 1 capsule at night.

Black cohosh, damiana, dong quai, and ginseng are the four most commonly used herbs to reduce menopausal symptoms.

Black Cohosh

The dark root of this useful herb is often taken to help cool down hot flashes and relieve vaginal dryness. Used by native American women for gynecological problems and childbirth, it has estrogenic qualities and acts as a sedative to contract the uterus. It contains calcium, potassium, magnesium, and iron. Black cohosh also goes by the names squaw root and snakeroot.

Damiana

Damiana balances women's hormones and is particularly effective in dealing with hot flashes, anxiety, and nervousness. It is also known as a sexual stimulant to help restore interest and capacity.

Dong Quai

Traditionally prescribed by Chinese doctors, dong quai is the herb that shows up in most herbal combinations for female complaints, commonly taken to diminish hot flashes. Acupuncturist Teresa Xu says, "Dong quai is also effective as a blood purifier and helps improve circulation. It nourishes the blood and helps keep women calm when their hormones are changing."

Author Diane Stein[17] says, "Dong quai is the women's ginseng, and . . . is *primary* in treating the symptoms of menopause, including hot flashes. It is an estrogen precursor—a source for estrogen—but it is not an estrogen itself." Ms. Stein also says that "some women have difficulty in taking dong quai. They experience nervousness like an exaggerated PMS. If this is the case for you, stop it and switch to black cohosh, which does similar things but is a progesterone precursor."

Ginseng

Three forms of ginseng are available in this country: Chinese, Korean, and Siberian. Herbalists have their preferences, but, in fact, all three perform similarly. In China ginseng is the herb that is said to cure "everything," but it is used mostly by older people to slow the process of aging and increase energy by improving circulation and strengthening the heart. Gelen or Jillin ginseng is a particularly effective form, highly prized by Chinese herbalists but very expensive (see Dr. Corsello, page 22). The Chinese also use ginseng for menopausal problems, to prevent disease, to normalize blood pressure, and to reduce cholesterol. Ginseng can help stimulate the immune system, corrects hormonal imbalance, has an anticlotting effect that reduces the risk of heart attack, and also helps people deal with stress. Ginseng can protect the liver from the effects of alcohol or drugs and contains vitamins A, E, and B_{12} and calcium, as well as other important vitamins and minerals. Ginseng comes in different strengths, so it is best to consult an herbalist for the most effective type for your body.

In their 1987 book,[18] Patsy Westcott and Leyardia Black, N.D., recommend taking "600 mg to 1200 mg" of ginseng.

Other herbs used to treat the range of symptoms that occur during and after menopause are alfalfa, angelica, blessed thistle, buchu, chasteberry, elder, false unicorn, lady's slipper and passion flower, licorice root and sarsaparilla, motherwort, pennyroyal, shepherd's purse, squaw vine, valerian, and wild yam.

Alfalfa

Alfalfa is an effective herb for menopausal symptoms. As a blood purifier, it cleanses the body and fights infection. It helps eliminate that bloated feeling by relieving water retention and works to lessen heavy periods.

Angelica

Angelica is used as a tonic for women in menopause to relieve tiredness, headaches, and anxiety. It also contains vitamin E and calcium, both useful when hormone levels are changing.

Blessed Thistle

This herb is used as a tonic to enhance the whole body. It is also good for helping to relieve menstrual disorders and as well as headaches.

Buchu

The leaves of the buchu plant are used in herbal medicine as a mild antiseptic and an antibacterial. During menopause and after, when women have problems with leaking or irritated bladders or problems with the urethra, buchu is recommended, singly or in combination with other herbs like juniper berries, couch grass, and uva-ursi.

Chasteberry

In *Menopause News,*[19] Anna Harvey, a licensed chiropractor who studied herbs at the California School of Herbal Studies, discussed chasteberry. Ms. Harvey says it was "named by monks in the Mediterranean, where it grows naturally. Because it is a female hormone that balances the system, the monks used it to reduce libido. In some women chasteberry acts like estrogen, in others like progesterone."

Elder

The flower and berries of this useful herb detoxify the body and purify the blood, and act as a sedative to calm the body and relieve pain. Elder is often used in combination with other herbs to fight infection.

False Unicorn

Used by many herbologists to treat the problems of the reproductive system, false unicorn is an effective general herb used by women in menopause to lift their spirits. It stimulates the reproductive organs, helps in uterine disorders, headaches, and depression.

Lady's Slipper and Passion Flower

Time and again, herbalists and naturopaths in alternative medicine literature recommend that lady's slipper and passion flower be used together to balance emotions, calm the body, and lighten states of anxiety and depression.

Lady's slipper, a gentle herb, is often used alone to calm a stressed nervous system. Frayed nerves and slight hysteria are common symptoms of menopause and can be eased by using lady's slipper.

Passion flower is also recommended for its calming effect on the nervous system. It helps to relieve insomnia and the physical and emotional stresses caused by lack of sleep.

Licorice Root and Sarsaparilla

Licorice root and sarsaparilla root are also recommended to be used together particularly to treat hot flashes because licorice is an herbal source for the hormone estrogen, while sarsparilla contains progesterone, the male hormone testosterone, and cortin—secretions of the adrenal cortex, the external layers of the adrenal gland—to help achieve glandular balance. Licorice stimulates the adrenal glands and helps increase energy levels and decrease stress. But it's important to note that licorice can raise blood pressure. Sarsaparilla increases the metabolic rate and helps improve circulation.

Motherwort

In *The Natural Remedy Book for Women,* Diane Stein talks about motherwort as the "herb of choice" if you decide to stop using synthetic hormones. Coming off hormonal therapy, your body can be in a state of hormonal imbalance unless you find some way to ease the transition. Consult a naturopath or nutritionist for more specific guidance.

Pennyroyal

Pennyroyal is used to treat a variety of female problems. It promotes menstruation and quiets the nerves.

Shepherd's Purse

Heavy menstrual periods are often relieved by using this herb, which helps to constrict blood vessels. Made from the whole plant, it contains vitamins C, E, and K as well as iron and calcium, among other minerals.

Squaw Vine

This herb, commonly used to strengthen the uterus during childbirth, is also used to help bring on a menstrual period. An herbal tranquilizer, it helps the kidneys eliminate urine, calms nerves, and is effective in treating vaginal infections.

Valerian

This herbal tranquilizer calms nerves with no side effects. It can focus your attention without causing drowsiness, and it helps to relieve anxiety safely. I use this herb quite often in a tincture, and from personal experience I know it works. Eight drops helps me concentrate, fifteen drops helps me relax enough to sleep.

Wild Yam

Often used to treat nausea in pregnancy, wild yam can help relieve menstrual cramps and calm nerves. Mexican yam specifically is an important ingredient in a natural progesterone cream, combined with soy-bean products and sometimes animal sources.

John R. Lee, M.D., reports in his paper *Osteoporosis Reversal*[20] that this natural progesterone may also be the "missing ingredient for normal bone building in women"—a subject of great importance for women concerned about osteoporosis. For six years Dr. Lee has conducted research on the use of transdermal natural progesterone supplementation—3 percent natural progesterone cream applied twice daily, one-half ounce a month. "Treatment resulted in progressive increase in bone mineral density and, more important, definite clinical improvement, including fracture prevention. The benefits achieved were found to be independent of age. It is concluded that osteoporosis reversal is a clinical reality in a program that is safe, uncomplicated, and inexpensive."

Although his study was based primarily on a balanced estrogen-progesterone program, there is a 1991 addendum to his paper: "Over one-third of the progesterone-treated patients in the study group received no supplemental estrogens. During the course of the study it was obvious that the *bone building benefits of the progesterone therapy* were independent of the presence or absence of supplemental estrogen." He goes on to say that natural progesterone therapy produced no side effects.

Women who can't or don't want to use hormones and are concerned about developing osteoporosis should consider using this natural progesterone program as an alternative.

Other aspects of the protocol in Dr. Lee's six-year study included a diet that emphasized leafy green vegetables. Sodas were eliminated, and red meat was limited to no more than three times a week. Alcohol was limited, and no cigarettes were allowed. The women took 350–400 IU of vitamin D every day, 2000 mg of vitamin C in divided doses each day, 15 mg daily of beta-carotene, 800–1000 mg of calcium daily by diet and/or supplements. The women in his study also exercised twenty minutes daily or one-half hour three times a week. (See interview with Dr. Serafina Corsello, who recommends the use of Progest Cream for menopausal patients, page 31.)

Herb Combinations

Herbalists often develop their own general combinations, using some of the herbs listed above and other herbs that are not designated specifically for menopause. These combinations may work as is, or the dosages may have to be adjusted for individual differences.

Dr. Andrew Weil, in his comprehensive manual for wellness and health care, *Natural Health, Natural Medicine,*[21] recommends an herbal formula for hot flashes that you can mix together yourself from capsules and tinctures. The herbs he recommends are dong quai, damiana, and chaparral (the leaves of the desert plant chapparal have strong antioxidant qualities): "Take two capsules of each of these herbs once a day at noon or one dropperful of each of the tinctures mixed in a cup of warm water (also) once a day at noon. This formula is safe and effective. Continue it until you do not experience any more hot flashes, then cut the dose gradually and try to stop altogether."

Susan Lark, M.D., in her useful *Menopause Self-Help Book,*[22] offers three herbal formulas that she recommends for "optimal nutritional support for women suffering from menopause-related complaints."

> **Formula I:** For women with general menopause complaints—hot flashes, vaginal dryness. Dr. Lark notes that this formula is "widely available in health food stores through Schiff Products."

Blue cohosh
False unicorn root
Fennel
Anise
Blessed thistle

Formula II: For women in menopause who are fatigued and weak

Ginger
Cayenne pepper
Siberian ginseng (eleutherococcus)

Formula III: For anxiety, irritability, and insomnia

Valerian root
Catnip
Chamomile
Hops
Red raspberry leaf

Dr. Lark recommends using Formula I as the basic treatment, adding Formula II and/or III if applicable to your symptoms.

In *Today's Herbal Health*[23], Louise Tenney offers the following herbal combination for menopause: black cohosh, licorice, false unicorn, Siberian ginseng, sarsaparilla, squaw vine, and blessed thistle (see pages 199–205 for individual descriptions of herbs).

A medical columnist in *Harper's Queen* magazine in Great Britain discussed Athera, an herbal remedy containing parsley, vervain, cleavers, and senna leaf that is "being touted as the natural alternative to hormone replacement therapy."

She says the product claims "to provide symptomatic relief for hot flushes, headaches, weight gain, and nervous tension." Athera herbal tablets are available in health food shops in England.

Vitamins and Minerals Useful for Menopause

Vitamins and minerals in a natural form are necessary to keep our bodies healthy and are particularly effective in preventing disease. During menopause, it is common to supplement vitamins and minerals because our bodies undergo such major changes. As Dr. Jeffrey Sullender points out, even a healthy diet may not give us the nutrients we need for energy and to maintain physical and emotional balance. Every active woman can probably use a high-quality multivitamin and mineral supplement, but if there is a need to take more of some specific vitamins, the resource book *Prescription for Nutritional Healing*[24] is a very useful self-help guide to vitamins, minerals, herbs, and food supplements.

Even if you choose to supplement, eating foods high in the vitamins you need makes sense. Consult the list of vitamins, with food sources, that are especially important for women during menopause. Try to add these foods to your normal diet; it may mean less supplementation.

The B Vitamins and Why They Are Important

Most experts recommend taking B complex vitamins, which include all the B's, but your practitioner may also suggest individual B vitamins as needed. In general, B's help sustain your nerves; keep your skin, hair, and eyes healthy; and strengthen your liver. They help ward off depression, anxiety, and stress and balance your energy. Most of us can benefit by taking the B vitamins not only at menopause, but as we grow older.

The most widely recommended treatment for stress is taking the B complex vitamins along with a good all-purpose multivitamin. The dosage of B's recommended by most experts is 50–100 mg three times a day.

Diane Stein *(The Natural Remedy Book for Women)* suggests, "You may also need additional B_6 (up to 50 mg three times a day), B_5 (100–500 mg two or three times a day), and/or PABA for adrenal function and stress. B_6 decreases water retention and menopause symptoms, with more needed if you are taking estrogen. B_5 aids adrenal function."

The individual B vitamins provide different benefits, and when you take a B complex pill daily, you get everything. However, it's important to know the work each B vitamin provides on its own.

Vitamin B_1 (Thiamine)

Vitamin B_1 is necessary for healthy blood formation and circulation. It energizes the central nervous system and helps maintain muscle tone in the heart and stomach. Natural vegetable sources for thiamine exist in brown rice, dried beans, peas, soy beans, wheat germ, whole grains, broccoli, brussels sprouts, peanuts, and raisins.

Vitamin B_2 (Riboflavin)

Riboflavin encourages red blood cell formation and strengthens the immune system by producing antibodies and aiding in cell metabolism. It also helps metabolize carbohydrates, fats, and proteins. Vitamin B_2 can lighten depression and lessen physical exhaustion. Skin, nails, and hair are all enhanced by this important vitamin. Spinach, beans, asparagus, broccoli, and brussels sprouts contain vitamin B_2.

Vitamin B_3 (Niacin)

Niacin is necessary for healthy circulation and enables the nervous system to function effectively. It helps metabolize carbohydrates, fats, and protein, aids digestion, and lowers cholesterol. Stress and insomnia can be relieved by using this vital B. Broccoli, carrots, potatoes, tomatoes, and whole wheat contain niacin.

Vitamin B_5 (Pantothenic Acid)

Known as the antistress vitamin, pantothenic acid helps produce adrenal hormones (steroids and cortisone) and aids in developing the antibodies that do the work of the immune system. B_5 also metabolizes fats, carbohydrates, protein, and vitamins and turns them into energy. B_5 helps the gastrointestinal tract to function normally. For menopausal women, this vitamin can be used to relieve anxiety, depression, and fatigue; lessen headaches; and slow down hair loss. Good sources for this B vitamin are beans, fresh vegetables, whole wheat, and saltwater fish.

Vitamin B_6 (Pyridoxine)

This essential vitamin influences more body functions than any other. The brain cannot function without B_6, and its presence is required by the nervous system. Pyridoxine promotes the production of red blood cells, aids in the synthesis of RNA and DNA (both essential for cell reproduction and growth), and helps immunize the body against cancer. Using this vitamin can reduce water retention and relieve, or even end, leg cramps. Those who take chemical estrogen may need to supplement to their diet with extra vitamin B_6. Foods containing the highest amounts of vitamin B_6 include brewer's yeast, carrots, spinach, sunflower seeds, and wheat germ. Chicken, eggs, fish, and meat are also very rich in this vitamin.

Vitamin B_{12} (Cyanocobalamin)

Preventing anemia by forming cells and blood is this vitamin's most important role. B_{12} also protects the body against nerve damage and digestive problems. It can help the body absorb food and synthesize protein while metabolizing carbohydrates and fats. The possibility of a vitamin B_{12} deficiency increases with age, particularly for those troubled by digestive problems. Vegetarians often take a B_{12} supplement because the vitamin is found primarily in animal sources. Tofu, made with soybeans, is the only vegetable source. Cheese, clams, eggs, herring, mackerel, milk, seafood, kidneys, and liver also contain vitamin B_{12}.

Biotin, Choline, Inositol, Folic Acid, and PABA

Biotin, another B vitamin, is produced in the body and synthesized in the intestines from food such as soy beans, whole grains, yeast, cooked egg yolk, fish, poultry, and meat. It metabolizes carbohydrates, fats, and proteins as well as all the B complex vitamins. Biotin is needed for healthy hair and skin and encourages development of healthy sweat glands, nerves, and bone marrow. Using chemical estrogen could deplete the body of biotin.

Choline combined with inositol becomes lecithin. Choline promotes hormone production and stronger brain and memory function; encourages red blood cell production; helps strengthen the nervous system; works to prevent hardening of the arteries; regulates the functioning of both the liver and the gallbladder; and aids in metabolizing fats and cholesterol. Whole-grain cereals and legumes are good sources of choline.

Inositol shares responsibility with choline for metabolizing fat and cholesterol; it, too, prevents hardening of the arteries and encourages active brain functioning. Inositol is vital for slowing hair loss and preventing skin problems and is an important vitamin for women during menopause. Coffee drinkers may need extra inositol, since caffeine can deplete the body's supply. Natural sources of inositol are the basis of a healthy diet for women at any time—vegetables, fruits, and whole grains.

Folic acid is essential for producing red blood cells needed for energy. Healthy cell division and cell reproduction is a second important function. Folic acid is a brain food and is useful for counteracting depression and anxiety. Beans, barley, legumes, bran, brewer's yeast, root and green leafy vegetables, and whole grains are all natural sources of folic acid.

PABA is now familiar to almost everyone as the antioxidant present in most sun preparations to prevent sunburn and skin cancer. PABA is one of the basic ingredients in folic acid and helps to form red blood cells and assist the body in assimilating protein. Nutritional experts recommend supplementing the diet with PABA to restore natural color to graying hair. Among food sources for PABA are whole grains and molasses.

The All-important Vitamin C

The antioxidant vitamin C is essential for women during menopause. Whether taken through food or through supplementation, its protective qualities cannot be overrated. At a time when the adrenals take over estrogen production from the ovaries, vitamin C encourages strong adrenal function. It also helps build white cells and strengthens the immune system. Vitamin C helps reduce heavy menstrual flow, and according to some experts, it relieves hot flashes. Daily dosages range from 2000 mg. to 4000 mg daily, depending on your body's tolerance.

Megadoses of vitamin C can end colds and infections as well as improve the physical condition of people with serious disease. Megadosing C on your own is not recommended, however; talk with your doctor first. Using prescription or over-the-counter drugs, drinking alcohol, or smoking can affect the amount of C you need.

Recently there have been new developments in vitamin C formulation. For example, ester C, a form of the vitamin, has made it possible to increase the amounts taken without loss through urine (a common problem with vitamin C). The body cannot manufacture vitamin C but needs it to function normally, so it must be provided by diet or vitamin pills or capsules. Vitamin C is found naturally in citrus fruits; green vegetables like broccoli, brussels sprouts, Swiss chard, kale, and beet greens; and mangos, papayas, and melons.

Vitamin D

Maintaining strong bones and teeth at any age depends on vitamin D and calcium, but after menopause women need vitamin D to prevent osteoporosis. The sun is the natural source for vitamin D, but many women stay out of the sun, choosing to supplement rather than risk skin cancer. Supplemental D should be taken with calcium to allow the body to metabolize it through the liver and kidneys.

Vitamin E

This vitamin is particularly useful and effective for women during and after menopause: as a supplement it can lessen hot flashes, and in a liquid form applied directly to the vaginal area, it counteracts dryness. Vitamin E also helps in blood circulation and assists in blood clotting. Vitamin E is found abundantly in the foods of a healthy vegetarian diet: cold-pressed vegetable oils, beans, legumes, brown rice, whole grains, dark green leafy vegetables, nuts, and seeds.

The dosages for taking vitamin E internally, for vaginal dryness and hot flashes, range from 30 IU to 600 IU, the top safe dosage level; 100 IU seems to be an average starting point. Most experts recommend experimenting to find the lowest level that works for you. Women with diabetes or high blood pressure should limit vitamin E intake to 100 IU. If you are under medical care for any serious condition, talk with your doctor or alternative practitioner about how much vitamin E to use before starting on a program. Be patient; it takes time to work, sometimes as long as a month, even if used daily.

According to Westcott and Black *(Alternative Health Care for Women),* if you take vitamins C and the B complex and ginseng along with the vitamin E, it "seems to improve the action."

In her book *Menopause: a Positive Approach,*[25] Rosetta Reitz says, "Many women have found relief [from hot flashes] in two days from taking 800 IU of vitamin E complex, also known as mixed tocopherols. Hot flashes disappear completely when vitamin E is also accompanied by 2000 to 3000 mg vitamin C (taken at intervals throughout the day) and with 1000 mg (also at intervals) of calcium from dolomite or bone meal. When the flashes have subsided, usually after a week, the women reduce the vitamin E intake to 400 IU."

Calcium/Magnesium/Boron

Calcium is the one mineral most women know about, the one strongly recommended by most doctors and alternative practitioners (see interviews with Jeffrey Sullender, page 108, who is one exception, and Serafina Corsello, page 22. Most experts say we need 700–1000 mg calcium a day before menopause and 1000–1500 for the rest of our lives, but consult with your doctor or alternative practitioner on the amount your body needs. (If you are taking calcium specifically to prevent osteoporosis, without the use of estrogen, weight-bearing exercise is equally essential.) Magnesium is needed by the body for proper absorption of calcium, but the amount needed depends on various factors such as a woman's diet and the levels of physical and emotional stress in her life. Natural sources for calcium include dairy products, salmon and sardines with bones, seafood, and green leafy vegetables. Molasses and brewer's yeast are also good sources, along with nuts and seeds and yogurt.

Drinking alcohol can interfere with the body's metabolism of calcium, and caffeine or salt taken in large quantities will eliminate calcium from your body, so it's wise to moderate the use of all three.

Boron, too, is an important factor in this equation. In *Prescription for Nutritional Healing,* Dr. James Balch and Phyllis Balch say, "The latest study conducted by the U.S. Department of Agriculture indicated that within eight days of supplementing the diet with 3 mg of boron, a test group of postmenopausal women lost 40 percent less calcium, [and] one-third less magnesium."

Essential Oils

In *The Menopause Self-Help Book,*[26] Dr. Lark discusses essential fatty acids and their importance to women during menopause. Two special fatty acids, linoleic and linolenic, cannot be made by the body and need to be supplied through food or by taking supplements. (See Dr. Sullender, page 108.)

Dr. Lark says, "Essential oils are particularly important to menopausal women because the deficiency of these oils is responsible in part for the drying of the skin, hair, vaginal tissues, and other mucous membranes that occurs with menopause. Along with vitamin E, which also benefits the skin and vaginal tissues, I have used essential oils extensively in my nutritional programs for women."

She goes on to say that "the average healthy adult requires only four teaspoons per day of the essential oils in their diet. However, menopausal women with extremely dry skin, hair, and vaginal tissues may have a real deficiency of these oils and need up to two to three tablespoons per day until their symptoms improve." Again, Dr. Lark says Schiff Products distributes this supplement through health food stores. Her essential formula consists of flax oil, borage oil, wheatgerm oil, fish oil (omega-3), and vitamin E.

Evening primrose oil, neither herb nor vitamin, comes up occasionally in the literature on menopause alternatives, but editor Janine O'Leary Cobb, in her information-packed newsletter, *A Friend Indeed,*[27] says that many women find evening primrose oil capsules "effective in reducing or eliminating hot flashes." She qualifies it, though, by saying, "Most of the studies I've seen that involve evening primrose oil have been produced by Dr. David Horrobin, who is the director of the Efamol Research Institute. Efamol is the leading maker of evening primrose oil capsules."

Cell Salts

Cell salts, although technically a homeopathic remedy, are more likely to be recommended by naturopaths and herbalists than homeopathic practitioners.

The system of cell salts, developed by homeopath William Schuessler, is, I think, ideal for use by people interested in self-care. Schuessler developed twelve remedies based on the chemical composition of body cells. The package insert says, "These tissue salts are vital constituents of the body, the workers, the builders, which combine with organic substances in creating and maintaining the millions of cells of which the body is composed. Thus, any tissue-salt deficiency or imbalance may result in disease, the symptoms varying according to the salt which is lacking."

The following are indications for using the cell salts, again taken from the package insert. Several of the women we interviewed use cell salts regularly to balance their bodies as part of their program for menopause. Cell salts can be dissolved under the tongue; they have a slightly sweet taste and are not difficult to use. Most health food stores stock cell salts, which are generally regarded as nutritional supplements. The cell salts marked with asterisks in the list that follows are often used by women to deal with bodily changes at menopause.

Diane Stein suggests the following cell salts for hot flashes: "Kali. Sulph., Kali. Phos., and Ferr. Phos. Take five tablets of each hourly until the condition improves, then use twice a day." She recommends the same dosage of Kali. Phos. with Nat. Mur. "for nervousness and emotional symptoms."

Calc. Fluor. (calcium fluoride)*: elastic tissue builder. For relaxed conditions of elastic fibers and blood vessels, muscular weakness, impaired circulation, piles, deficient enamel of teeth, cracks in the skin, bone bruises, and varicose veins.

Calc. Phos. (calcium phosphate)*: general nutrient, appropriate for chilblains, simple anemia, impaired digestion, malassimilation, infants' teething troubles. The ideal tonic.

Calc. Sulph. (calcium sulphate): blood purifier. Minor skin ailments, acne, pimples during adolescence.

Ferr. Phos. (ferric phosphate): oxygen carrier. Coughs, colds, chills, inflammation, congestion, fevers, headaches. The preeminent biochemic first aid.

Kali. Mur. (potassium chloride): blood conditioner. Coughs, colds, chills, bronchitis, catarrh (alternate with Ferr. Phos.). The children's remedy.

Kali. Phos. (potassium phosphate)*: nerve nutrient. Nervous exhaustion, nervous indigestion, nervous headaches.

Kali. Sulph. (potassium sulphate)*: oxygen exchanger. Minor skin eruptions with scaling, bronchial catarrh, evening aggravation of symptoms.

Mag. Phos. (magnesium phosphate)*: nerve stabilizer. Spasmodic darting pains, cramp, neuralgia, flatulence.

Nat. Mur. (sodium chloride)*: water distributor. Dryness or excessive moisture in any part of the body. Running watery colds with loss of smell or taste.

Nat. Phos. (sodium phosphate): acid neutralizer. Acidity, digestive upsets, heartburn, rheumatic pain.

Nat. Sulph. (sodium sulphate): excess water eliminator. Liverishness, biliousness, influenza, watery infiltrations. The liver salt.

Silica (silicic oxide)*: cleanser. Impure blood, boils, pus formation, brittle nails, lackluster hair (alternate with kali. sulph.).

Miscellaneous Remedies for Symptoms

Melbrosia: Bee Pollen and Royal Jelly in Pill Form

According to Janine Cobb in her newsletter, *A Friend Indeed,*[28] thirty-five of thirty-eight women tested by a gynecologist in Ljubljana, Yugoslavia, "claimed that all their menopausal complaints disappeared after being on bee pollen and royal jelly tablets for two months. Another test in Germany is said to confirm these findings." Ms. Cobb goes on to say that the tablets sold in Canada are called "Melbrosia pld . . . and the dose is one tablet daily. The price is $10.95 for fifteen tablets, Canadian currency."

In *Earth Rites,*[29] editor Sherry Mestel also recommends using the herb thyme, combined with hot water as a tea, to help regulate circulation. Cucumber juice, birch leaf tea, lavender tea, and rosemary tea are also useful for relieving menopausal symptoms in general. Diet suggestions include "more raw green vegetables, vitamins B_1, B_{12}, B_6, vitamin E, wheatgrass oil, and yeast to slow aging."

Deep Breathing Exercise for Hot Flashes

The August 1992 issue of *The American Journal of Obstetrics and Gynecology* presents a study on behavioral treatment of menopausal hot flashes designed with thirty-three women who have frequent hot flashes. The women were divided into three groups and received training in paced respiration (breathing exercises), muscle relaxation, or alpha-wave biofeedback. The results showed that when women were trained in slow, deep breathing exercises there was a significant reduction in hot flashes over a twenty-four-hour period, sleeping and awake. Alternative practitioners who have long recommended doing yoga breathing exercises to deal with stress can now point to concrete evidence that they also help diminish hot flashes.

Menopause News[30] offers some information on Replens, an over-the-counter product marketed specifically for women at midlife. Replens is "a moisturizing gel 'tampon' that is inserted into the vagina two or three times a week. It has the advantage of not being administered right before intercourse. Replens is a water-filled polymer that clings to cell walls and plumps them up. Some women, however, have complained that it balled up inside and require douching to remove it." (See Dr. Elmaleh, page 50.)

Betty Nickerson, author of *Old and Smart,*[31] mentions that "an effective lubricant has been developed by Doctor Marilyn Pratt. . . . It is called Creme de la Creme, marketed by Especially Products, Inc." Ms. Nickerson says it is excellent but difficult to find. The most current address she had for Especially Products is P.O. Box 5477, Playa del Rey, CA 90296.

Glandulars for Decreased Energy Level

As natural estrogen levels decrease, women begin to draw more heavily on the endocrine system, particularly the adrenals, causing hormonal imbalances. If they are also trying to sustain the same schedules of work and life-style pressures, they may experience bouts of fatigue and exhaustion. Some naturopaths as well as medical doctors recommend the use of glandulars like raw adrenal to promote adrenal function and increased thymus, pituitary, and reproductive gland performance. In their self-help guide,[32] the Balches state that physicians in Europe have used glandulars since the turn of the century to supplement the body's human cells with animal cells similar in function. However, Andrew Weil, M.D., author of *Natural Health, Natural Medicine,*[33] strongly "recommends against using these products." He believes that using "hormone supplements, in either synthetic or glandular tissue form, unless a definite need is established by appropriate medical tests," is "at best . . . unnecessary, at worst dangerous." He reasons that the body's hormonal system is very delicate and that women should be cautious about taking anything that can upset that balance. Recognizing that the use of glandulars (a popular natural supplement recommended for menopausal women today) elicits such strong opposing views, women should find out more about them if they are considering self-prescription. Seek advice from your doctor or alternative practitioner and find out if your body needs this supplement.

Notes

Introduction

1. Page xviii. September 17, 1983, "Estrogen Trials and Errors."

Part One: Natural Menopause

2. Page 4. July 28, 1993, *The New York Times.*
3. Page 14. Sources: Teaching Atlas, Breast Ultrasound, Wolfgang Leuct (George Thiem, Stuttgart, 1992), and Robert Bard, M.D., *N.Y. State Journal of Medicine,* February 1993.

Part Two: Alternative Approaches

4. Page 49. *Holistic Medicine,* Henry Edward Altenberg, M.D. Japan Publishing, 1992.
5. Page 55. *Homeopathic Medicine for Women,* Trevor Smith, M.D. Healing Arts Press, Worcester, Vermont, 1989.
6. Page 56. *The Natural Remedy Book for Women,* The Crossing Press, Freedom, California, 95019.
7. Page 56. Dr. Brigitte Borho, dr. rer. nat., in an article for *Biologische Medzen* 29/4km, 1991, and reprinted in *Biological Therapy1* volume X/no. 2, 1992.
8. Page 68. April 1990.
9. Page 75. Helene McLean, in her chapter, "Alternative Therapies," in *Everywoman's Health.* Simon & Schuster, fifth ed., 1993.
10. Page 75. J. J. Augustin Publisher, coauthored with William John Miller.

Part Three: Women Who Manage Menopause Naturally

11. Page 143. Phillip M. Chancellor, The C. W. Daniel Company, Ltd., 60 Muswell Road, London, N.10, England, 1971.
12. Page 146. Paavo Airola, M.D., Ph.D., Health Plus Publishers.
13. Page 146. James Balch, M.D., and Phyllis A. Balch, C.N.C., Avery Publishing Group.
14. Page 149. According to James Bache, M.D., and Phyllis Bache, C.N.C., *Prescription for Nutritional Healing,* Avery Publishing, the following daily dosages for good health are recommended (but before using any supplement they suggest consulting your physician): vitamin A—10,000 IU; vitamin D—400 IU; vitamin E—600 IU.
15. Page 164. *Women Talk About Gynecological Surgery,* Gross/Ito, Clarkson Potter Publishing, 1990.
16. Page 169. Marian Van Eyck McCaine, Greenwood Publishing Group.

Part Four: More on Herbs, Vitamins, and Supplements

17. Page 201. *The Natural Remedy Book for Women,* Crossing Press, Berkeley, California, 1992 (page 249).
18. Page 202. Thorsons Publishing Group, Rochester, Vermont (page 148).
19. Page 203. May/June 1991. *Menopause News* is a well-researched newsletter published six times a year out of San Francisco (1-800-24-MENO).
20. Page 205. Published in the *International Clinical Nutrition Review,* June 1990; Sydney, Australia.
21. Page 207. Houghton Mifflin, 1990 (pages 308–309).
22. Page 207. *Menopause Self-Help Book,* Celestial Arts Publishing, Berkeley, California, 1990 (page 130).
23. Page 208. Woodland Books, Provo, Utah; Third Edition, 1992 (page 232).
24. Page 209. James F. Balch, M.D. and Phyllis A. Balch, C.N.C., Avery Publishing.
25. Page 215. Chilton Book Company, 1977.
26. Page 217. (pages 105–107).
27. Page 217. Volume II, No 6, November 1985.
28. Page 220. Volume II, No 6, November 1985.

29. Page 220. Volume I *Herbal Remedies,* Earth Rites Press, Brooklyn, New York.
30. Page 221. January/February, 1992.
31. Page 221. All About Us Books, U.S.A. & Canada, 1991 (page 238).
32. Page 222. *Prescription for Nutritional Healing.*
33. Page 222. Houghton Mifflin, 1990.

Resources

Organizations

American Aromatherapy Association
P.O. Box 1222
Fair Oaks, California 95628

American Association of Acupuncture and Oriental Medicine
1424 16th Street N.W., #501
Washington DC 20036
(202)265-2287

American Association of Naturopathic Physicians
P.O. Box 20386
Seattle, Washington
98112

American Center for the Alexander Technique, Inc.
129 West 67th Street
New York, New York
10023
(212) 799-0468

American Chiropractic Association
1701 Clarendon Blvd.
Arlington, Virginia 22209

American College of Traditional Chinese Medicine
455 Arkansas Street
San Francisco, California 94107

American Herb Association
P.O. Box 353
Rescue, California 95672

American Holistic Medical Association
4101 Lake Boone Trail, Suite 201
Raleigh, North Carolina 27607
(919) 787-5146

American Society of Clinical Hypnosis
2250 East Devon Avenue, Suite 336
Des Plaines, Illinois 60018
(312) 297-3317

Bach Centre
Mount Vernon
Stowell
Wallingford
Oxon OX10PZ
England

The Feldenkrais Guild
P.O. Box 13285
Overland Park, Kansas 66212-3285 USA
(913) 492-1444
FAX (913) 492-0955

Flower Essence Society
P.O. Box 1769
Nevada City, California
95959

Homeopathic Educational Services
22124 Kittridge Street

Berkeley, California
94704
(415) 547-2492

International College of Applied Kinesiology
P.O. Box 25276
Shawnee Mission, Kansas 66225

International College of Applied Kinesiology
P.O. Box 680547
Park City, Utah 84068

International Foundation of Homeopathy
2366 Eastlake E.
Seattle, Washington 98102
(206) 324-8230

International Institute of Reflexology
P.O. Box 12642
St. Petersburg, Florida
33733-2642

Menopause News
(800)241-MENO
A newsletter for information on new developments in the treatment of menopausal symptoms.

National Center for Homeopathy
801 N. Fairfax Street
Suite 306
Alexandria, Virginia 22314
(703) 548-7790

National College of Naturopathic Medicine
11231 S.E. Market Street
Portland, Oregon 97216

National Women's Health Network
1325 G Street N.W.
Washington, D.C. 20006
(202) 223-2226

North American Society of Teachers of The Alexander Technique
P.O. Box 3992
Champaign, Illinois
61826-3992
(217) 359-3529

Pacific Institute of Aromatherapy
P.O. Box 606
San Rafael, California 94915
(415) 459-3998

Natural Health Professionals

Serafina Corsello, M.D.
200 West 57th Street
New York, New York
10019
(212) 399-0222

Melanie Danza
New York University Women's Wellness Center
317 East 34th Street
4th Floor
New York, New York
10016
(212) 263-6363
(914) 764-0833

Rebecca Elmaleh, M.D.
103 Fifth Avenue
New York, New York
10003
(212)229-9718

Marcia Greenleaf, Ph.D.
19 East 88th Street
New York, New York
10128
(212) 534-8877

Christine Henrich, M.T.
P.O. Box 156
New York, New York
10014
(212) 691-0929

Roberta Kirchenbaum
316 West 94th Street
New York, New York
10025
(212) 222-7396

Neil Kobetz, D.C.
430 East 86th Street
New York, New York
10028
(212) 628-8500

Loretta Mears, D.C.
80 East 11th Street
Suite 501
New York, New York
10003
(212) 353-2188

Marika Molnar, P.T.
Westside Physical Therapy
2101 Broadway
New York, New York
(212) 799-0160

Sarnell Ogus
49 Sandra Road
East Hampton, New York
11937
(516) 324-6218
New York, New York
10021
(212) 242-1188

Jeffrey Sullender, Ph.D., C.C.N.
Nutrition Research and Health Center
of New Hampshire
39 Simon Street
Suite 3A
Nashua, New Hampshire
03060
(603) 881-8300

Teresa Xu
250 West 57th Street
Suite 1202
New York, New York
10107-1202
(212) 245-3372

Bibliography

Acupressure for Women
Cathryn Bauer, The Crossing Press, 1987

The Alexander Technique
Selected and introduced by Edward Maisel
First Carol Publishing Group, 1990
A Lyle Stewart Book

Alternative Health Care for Women
Patsy Westcott and Leyardia Black, N.D.
Thorsons Publishing Group, Wellingsborough, Northamptonshire,
Rochester, Vermont, 1987

Better Health Through Natural Healing
Dr. Ross Trattler
McGraw-Hill Book Company, 1985

Biological Therapy
Volume X/No. 2, 1992
Therapy of the Menopausal Syndrome with Mulimen—Results of a
Multicentric Post-Marketing Survey

Chinese Herbal Medicine
Daniel P. Reid
Shambhala Publications, Inc.
Boston, Massachusetts, 1992

Conn's Current Therapy, 1991
W. B. Saunders Company
Harcourt Brace Jovanovich, Inc.

Encyclopedia of Natural Medicine
Michael Murray, N.D., and Joseph Pizzorno, N.D.
Prima Publishing, Rocklin, California, 1991

The Essential Guide to Vitamins and Minerals
Elizabeth Somer, M.A., R.D.
Harper Perennial, New York, 1992

Essential Supplements for Women
Carolyn Reuben, C.A., and Joan Priestley, M.D., Perigree Books by Putnam Publishing, 1988

Estrogen: Is it Right for You?
Paula Dranov, Simon & Shuster, 1993

Estrogen—The Facts Can Change Your Life
Lila Nachtigall, M.D., and Joan Rattner Heilman
The Body Press, 1986

Everywoman's Health
D. S. Thomson, M.D., consulting editor,
Fireside/Simon & Schuster, 1980, 1982, 1985, 1993

Exercise in the Menopausal Woman
Mona Shangold, M.D.
Obstetrics and Gynecology, volume 75, no. 4 (supplement), April 1990

Handbook of the Bach Flower Remedies
Phillip M. Chancellor
The C. W. Daniel Company Ltd.
1971

Health and Healing
Andrew Weil, M.D.
Houghton Mifflin Company, Boston, Massachusetts, 1988

Health Through Balance
Dr. Yeshi Donden
Snow Lion Publications
Ithaca, New York 1986

Herbally Yours
Penny C. Royal
Sound Nutrition, Hurricane, Utah, 1982

Hiatal Hernia Syndrome
Theodore A. Baroody, Jr., M.A., D.C.
Eclectic Press, Waynesville, North Carolina

Holistic Medicine
Henry Edward Altenberg, M.D.
Japan Publications, 1992

Homeopathic Medicine for Women
Trevor Smith, M.D.
Healing Arts Press, Rochester, Vermont, 1984

Making the Estrogen Decision
Gretchen Henkel
RGA Publishing Group, 1992

The Medical Self-Care Book of Women's Health
Bobbie Hasselbring, Sadja Greenwood, M.D., M.P.H., Michael Castleman
Doubleday & Company, Inc., Garden City, New York 1987

Menopause, Naturally
Sadja Greenwood, M.D.
Volcano Press, 1989

Menopause News
Jan./Feb. 1992
Newsletter
21074 Union Street
San Francisco, California 94123
1-800-241-MENO

The Menopause Self-Help Book
Susan M. Lark, M.D., Celestial Arts, 1990

Miracle Medicine Herbs
Richard M. Lucas
Parker Publishing, West Nyack, New York, 1991

Moderate Physical Activity and Bone Density among Perimenopausal Women
Jun Zhang, MB, Paul J. Feldblum, MSPH, and Judith A. Fortney, Ph.D.
Abstract, *The American Journal of Public Health,*
May 1992, volume 82, no. 5

Natural Healing in Gynecology
Rina Nissim
Pandora Press, Translation from the French, 1986

Natural Health, Natural Healing
Andrew Weil, M.D.
Houghton Mifflin Company, Boston, Massachusetts, 1988

The Natural Remedy Book for Women
Diane Stein
The Crossing Press, Freedom, California, 1992

New England Journal of Medicine
Editorial, October 24, 1985
"When Research Results Are in Conflict"

Prescription for Nutritional Healing
James F. Balch, M.D., Phyllis A. Balch, C.N.C.
Avery Publishing Group Inc., 1990

Return to Life
Joseph Pilates and William John Miller
J. J. Augustin Publisher, 1945

Second Spring
Honora Lee Wolfe, Blue Poppy Press, 1990

Taking Hormones and Women's Health:
Choices, Risks, Benefits
National Women's Health Network Publication, 1989
1325 G Street, N.W.
Washington, D.C. 2005

Today's Herbal Health
Louise Tenney, M.H.
Woodland Books, Provo, Utah, 1992

Index